CW01655650

Designated Teacher Guidebook

The definitive guide to being an effective designated teacher

Edited by
Clive Grimshaw
Matthew Huggins

With a foreword by
Professor Sonia Jackson OBE

Acknowledgements

Writing and producing this guidebook would not have been possible witout contributions from a number of people. The invaluable advice and guidance those individuals provided was essential to creating a guidebook that balanced the knowledge and skill of the teaching profession with the objective of this project; to offer the definitive guide to being an effective designated teacher. Care Matters Partnership would like to express gratitude and thanks to the following people who have acted as the review group for this project: Nick Peacey (Institute of Education), Professor Bob Broad (London South Bank University), Margery Brooke-Williams (London Borough of Barking and Dagenham), Mark Austin (Monteagle Primary School, Dagenham) and David Cohen (Psychology News).

Thanks also to Carl Packman, Clare Wenham and Katy Taylor at Care Matters Partnership for their hard work assisting in the editing process and to Mari Lindfors for her patience and skill in the designing of this guidebook. We would also like to thank all the looked after children and care leavers who work with us for their willingness to be honest and frank about their experiences of care and for offering equally honest and frank guidance on how it should be improved. This guidebook will take us one step closer to improving their lives.

A publication of this nature and importance also reflects the determination of professionals and academics who have worked tirelessly over the years to highlight the importance of improving the care and support provided to looked after children and care leavers. Care Matters Partnership acknowledges in particular the work of Professor Sonia Jackson OBE and Professor David Berridge OBE highlighting the need for better support in school, to Susanna Cheale OBE for her kind words of advice and to Kevin Woods and Michael Allured at the Department for Education for their commitment to working so openly and constructively with everyone in the children's sector to see through the improvements we all believe are the right ones.

Care Matters Partnership

Care Matters Partnership is a social enterprise with a mission to be the best provider of knowledge to professionals working with children. Care Matters Partnership is already well established as a leader in providing evidenced based solutions for improving workforce knowledge and productivity – helping professionals to deliver the best possible services to children, young people and adults. The Care Matters Partnership team are highly experienced in the sector as well as in the delivery of conferences, events, training and publications. Our staff have been involved in Government working groups, research groups and involved in the governance of several charities as trustees. Care Matters Partnership is supported by a range of sector specialists including academics, former service managers, directors and policy makers.

Published by Care Matters Partnership Ltd

Designed by Mari Lindfors
Printed by Catalyst Image Solutions
ISBN number 978-0-9565978-0-9

Care Matters Partnership is a limited company registered in England and Wales. Registered Number: 06763247; Registered Office: Acre House, 11/15 William Road, London NW1 3ER
www.carematterspartnership.co.uk

Academic advisor

Professor Bob Broad

Dr Bob Broad is Professor of Children and Families Research at London South Bank University in the Social Policy and Urban Research Institute (SPUR). He was previously Director of the National Children's Bureau's research and evaluation department. A qualified teacher and social worker, he has worked in many inner London boroughs as a teacher and probation officer before initially taking a lecturing role at the London School of Economics. He has recently undertaken research projects and reviews for the then Department of Children, Schools and Families, Save the Children, the Fostering Network, The Adolescent and Children's Trust and the Grandparents Association. His research interests include fostering, grandparenting, children leaving care, kinship care, international kinship care and young people's health and well being.

Editorial team

Matthew Huggins: Chief Executive Officer, Care Matters Partnership

Matthew Huggins has a track record of working at a strategic level on issues regarding the education of looked after children, including as a senior manager in private residential care and as a councillor. He is a regular speaker at conferences across the country, as a trustee for the British Association for Adoption and Fostering and The Caldecott Foundation and, more recently, as a member of the best practice in schools working group for the Care Matters: Time for Change White Paper. He is the author of *I'll Love You If...*, an autobiographical account of his own journey through care.

Clive Grimshaw: Head of Policy & Research, Care Matters Partnership

Clive has experience working across the political and professional aspects of local government. Previously working in children's policy at the Local Government Association, he brings expertise on the key Acts around looked after children, including the Children Act 1989, the Children Act 2004, and the Children and Young Persons Act 2008. At the Local Government Association, Clive also worked to influence and improve government policy and legislation, and was active in the development and implementation of the Care Matters: Time for Change programme. He also led child protection policy development, and shaped improvements to the child protection policy framework resulting from Lord Laming's report in 2009.

Liz Cheesbrough: Researcher, Care Matters Partnership

A BSc social policy and governance graduate from the London School of Economics, Liz has previously worked with young people and enjoys working on issues related to empowerment and participation.

James Hall: Researcher, Care Matters Partnership

Currently completing a MA in legal and political theory from the School of Public Policy at University College London, James's thesis focuses on the demands of equality and legitimacy in British education policy. Previously, he has taught English in a Chinese high school with the British Council, and worked as an educational playworker on a Hampshire County Council funded project in the New Forest area.

Preface

I founded Care Matters Partnership for two reasons. The first was my passion to change the lives of children and young people in care which I believe can be achieved by providing knowledge to teachers and children's social care professionals. The second was to realise my own lifelong aspiration to become an entrepreneur.

I am an unlikely chief executive of a leading organisation providing knowledge to professionals. Having spent the latter part of my childhood in care I left school and care at the age of sixteen with no qualifications. I started my career not in the lecture rooms of universities, nor through internships and graduate programmes, but in the kitchens of fast food outlets and the rough and tumble of trying to make the most of opportunities for a better life.

This was not because I wasn't academically minded – far from it - I relished the opportunity to go back to mainstream school after missing the last year of junior school and the first two years of secondary school. I remember my first day returning to secondary mainstream clearly. I was wearing my first ever school uniform with tie knotted tightly, shoes like a mirror and blazer buttoned up, chest puffed out. I was proud, excited and jubilant at the prospect of learning and reaching my potential. I knew then, as I had for several years, that I was going to go to university.

Then I arrived at school in a variety club minibus on the school run with all the other children from my children's home. Everybody immediately knew I was a child in care. My form group appeared to have been briefed about care status – with the intention of getting them to treat me lightly. It didn't work. Far from treating me lightly other children constantly quizzed me about my home life as if a circus act and others chose simply to abuse me verbally and physically.

The school seemed to give up on me far quicker than they did my non-cared for peers. It was easier to blame me as the problem child than tackle the bullying head on. There was no personal education plan to address the social issues in school that was holding me back academically. And no designated teacher to go and talk to about these problems. Some teachers would refer to my care status when they told me off in front of the class; others would privately tell bullies to lay off me because I had a sad life at home. I felt lonely, angry and sad throughout my time at mainstream school. By the age of fifteen, about six months before my GCSEs, I had been suspended many times and was finally expelled.

So what did enable me to go on and make a career for myself firstly in politics and then in business as the owner of two growing companies? It was many people and many things, but my teachers played a key role. Before I went to mainstream secondary I spent two years in the Caldecott Foundation school for looked after children. Unlike now, back then there was no national curriculum followed in schools. But the teachers at the school understood what we were going through in care, had daily contact with our residential staff and the home managers were intently engaged in the school's ethos and approach to working with each of us. I was treated as an individual and my own talents were recognised and respected.

Three teachers helped to change my life in particular. It was my class teacher, Valerie Lyon-Wall, who allowed me to express myself again and showed me unconditional support. It was my head teacher, Jonathan Stanley, who gave me £50 and an office to start the school newspaper, giving me my first experience of enterprise. And it was Peter, my art teacher, who taught me that I could achieve anything I wanted and showed me how to laugh again. What was most special about these people was the fact that they didn't judge me as a child in care; they worked with my carers but they didn't become an extension of that team, choosing instead to reach their own conclusions about me and provided me with a refuge from the chaos of my residential home life. This was lost when I went to mainstream school because I didn't have those people. But the impact they made on me changed my life; perhaps even saved it as I may have given up later in life had they not shown me those things they saw in me. I am still friends with all three now and am thankful they became teachers but even more thankful they decided to teach looked after children.

When I think about what a designated teacher should be I think of those three teachers. The designated teacher should be the person who believes in the child regardless of other peoples views, they should allow the child freedom to make mistakes and have an education separate to their home life, they should get to know the child and see things in them that not even the child does – but most of all they should have the passion and commitment to help that child be all they can be in life.

Care leavers will often tell you despite the many professionals in their life it is usually only one person that makes the life changing difference to them. That person could be you. And the difference you make as a designated teacher should not be underestimated – it can be the difference between life and death, as you will learn from the statistics in this book from the fates of too many care leavers. But it is more likely to be the difference between simply life – and living that life to its full potential.

This guidebook will help you, but after you have the knowledge the rest is about your tireless passion, commitment and absolute belief that every child in care can achieve the best of their potential. We wish you luck with that mission and we join you in it.

Matthew Huggins
Chief Executive
Care Matters Partnership

Foreword

Sonia Jackson OBE

Professor of Social Care and Education, Institute of Education, University of London

I remember once when I was a social worker being summoned to see a teacher who had asked for a child in her class who lived in a children's home to be moved to a special school. It soon became obvious that she disliked this little girl. None of the other children wanted to sit next to her because she quite often had an 'accident' at an age when such things are usually outgrown. After listening to a long list of complaints I asked "did you know that Josie has been moved 18 times since she came into care?" Miss Taylor said nothing, but her eyes filled with tears.

Two weeks later when I went back Josie seemed like a different child. She proudly showed me her reading book and told me "Miss is nice to me now". There was no more talk of special schools.

The recommendation in the 2000 joint guidance by the two responsible Departments that every school should appoint a member of staff to have a special role to promote the welfare and attainment of looked after children was a very significant forward step. Before that children in care were generally considered the responsibility of the SENCO (special educational needs coordinator) which sent a very negative message that being in foster or residential care was equivalent to having a learning disability. This certainly contributed to the low expectations which research has repeatedly identified as a major cause of the gap in achievement between looked after children and others.

Some teachers have always taken a sympathetic interest in children and young people looked after away from home, but the great majority know nothing of the care system and, like Miss Taylor, have little conception of the extremely disadvantaged homes from which the children come or the neglect and abuse they are likely to have suffered. Gaps in learning caused by irregular attendance can easily be misinterpreted as lack of ability. Embarrassment about literacy problems may manifest itself as 'laziness' or disruptive behaviour.

Initial teacher training does not usually include any sessions specifically about looked after children or the kinds of experiences that may make it difficult for them to cope in the classroom environment. This is often justified on the grounds that looked after children make up less than one per cent of the school population in most areas. However that argument would be considered completely unacceptable if applied to disabled children or those from minority ethnic backgrounds.

But the result is that many teachers still have negative and punitive attitudes towards looked after children which contribute to their high risk of exclusion, both from school, and later from society. So in addition to championing individual children, listening to their concerns and defending their interests, the designated teacher has the important job of informing and educating the rest of the staff group.

The small amount of research on how the designated teacher role is working shows that its effectiveness depends on three things: the seniority of the person undertaking the job, the amount of time allowed for it and access to information. All three can be problems. There is of course a huge amount of material on the web but what busy teacher has time to sort through it to find what is relevant?

This guidebook provides the essential information that a designated teacher needs to know in a succinct and accessible form. It will be an invaluable tool for designated teachers in all types of school and wherever they work. I wish it every success and hope it will be made widely available.

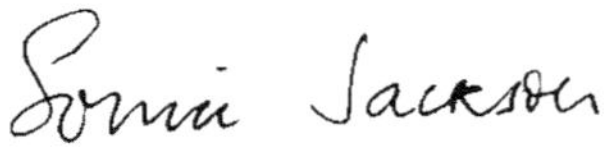

Professor Sonia Jackson OBE
29th May 2010

Introduction

We know that looked after children don't do as well as other children. This is particularly true in education where, for a number of reasons, looked after children have typically achieved far worse educational outcomes than their classmates.[1] This is shown in lower exam pass rates, poorer progress between key stages, and fewer looked after children going on to further and higher education.

Looked after children are not a homogenous group and it would be unfair to conclude that the reasons for under-achievement are the same from one child to the next. However, it would be even more unfair to assume that underachievement is a natural consequence of being looked after. In education, core support for raising the attainment of looked after children is provided by the looked after children education services and the 'virtual school' at the local authority level; and the designated teacher within the school. The designated teacher occupies one (albeit important) role in the larger team of professionals working towards helping the looked after child in all aspects of his or her development.

A brief history of the designated teacher role

In 2000, the Department of Health and the Department for Education and Employment (now the Department for Education) issued joint guidance on the Education of Young People in Public Care.[2] The report recommended that schools appoint a member of staff to act as a champion for looked after children within the school, using the same model as was already in place to allocate staff responsible for championing child protection and special educational needs issues.

Following the launch of the Care Matters: Time for Change policy programme in 2007, the government proposed the designated teacher should be made a statutory position, so that under law all schools must appoint a member of staff to the post. This proposal was approved and taken up in the Children and Young Persons Act 2008, which stated:

> **"The governing body of a maintained school must designate a member of staff at the school... as having responsibility for promoting the educational achievement of registered pupils at the school who... are looked after by a local authority."[3]**

Although there has since been statutory guidance for schools concerning the responsibilities of designated teachers, the post is relatively new, and designated teachers are often still finding their feet in the role. This book will help speed up that process - making it clearer and easier for designated teachers to know what their responsibilities are, and illustrating the best ways in which to fulfil them.

The importance of the designated teacher

As this book will illustrate, the designated teacher has the potential to be a powerful influence in helping looked after children achieve better results in school. The value of a good education, including good qualifications, is well-appreciated. All else being equal, a high-quality school experience provides

1 See e.g. DCSF (2010). Promoting the Educational Achievement of Looked After Children: Statutory Guidance for Local Authorities. Nottingham: DCSF Publications, p. 7.
2 DoH and DfEE (2000). Education of Young People in Public Care. London: DfEE.
3 The Children and Young Persons Act 2008, sec. 20(1).

access to a more fulfilling career, higher income, greater self-confidence and a better quality of life. This is obviously important for all children, but it gains extra weight for looked after children, who often already have the odds stacked against them because of their previous and ongoing experiences outside school.

The designated teacher plays a crucial role in ensuring looked after children have a positive experience of education. Through the personal contact he or she has with the looked after child, as well as in his or her relationship with school staff and with other professionals, the designated teacher is at the centre of all action to improve educational achievement. This book will provide the resources needed to support designated teachers to help looked after children get the most out of their time at school.

Notes to bear in mind when reading this guidebook

The use of the label 'looked after child'

Like most other labels, that of 'looked after child' is not always satisfactory. Many looked after children have reported that they dislike being categorised and singled out as such, and probably do not wish to be discussed in such an anonymous and impersonal fashion. However, for the sake of ease and clarity, the term 'looked after child' will be used throughout this book. The reader should note that the term was legally introduced by the Children's Act 1989, in which 'looked after' refers both to children subject to care orders made by the court and those who are voluntarily accommodated. Some local authorities use the terms 'children in care' or 'children looked after'.

To avoid confusion, it should also be noted that this book uses the terms 'actors', 'professionals' and 'practitioners' interchangeably to refer collectively to the diverse range of people and services that surround the looked after child.

Technical terms

Since the role bridges a number of areas of professional concern, the designated teacher is likely to encounter an array of specialised jargon. Where the reader is unsure of a term in the text - and it is not explained within the chapter - he or she should consult the glossary, at the end of the book. The glossary contains a comprehensive list of definitions and legal terminology and should function as a useful ongoing source of reference.

The information in this guidebook

This guidebook provides a rich mixture of facts, figures, legal explanations and case studies, as well as practical tips for helping designated teachers use the information provided effectively. The writers and editors have tried to keep guidebook accessible and to break information down into manageable sections. This includes using a number of themed text boxes throughout:

- 'Key information' boxes provide essential statistics and knowledge;
- 'What works well' boxes provide best practice examples; and
- 'What next?' boxes provide practical ideas on implementation, or signpost further information.

Laws and statutory guidance

The designated teacher's job, and the information concerning it in this book, is based in law, and it is important that all practitioners working with looked after children are familiar with their legal position. Three sources, though not exhaustive, are particularly useful in this regard:

- Children and Young Persons Act 2008.
- The Designated Teacher (Looked After Pupils etc)(England) Regulations 2009.

- The Role and Responsibilities of the Designated Teacher for Looked After Children: Statutory Guidance for School Governing Bodies.

What to do after reading this book

Looked after children are individuals with complex and unique life stories and it is not possible to cover all eventualities here. In addition, the designated teacher will need to keep up to date on changes in legislation and government policy, and informed of good practice. The governing body of the school has a statutory duty to ensure that designated teachers are supported with the appropriate training, and the materials in this book can be used as indicators for directing further professional development.

In aid of this process, Care Matters Partnership provides a range of online resources for designated teachers. These resources are available through the Care Matters Partnership website (www.carematterspartnership.co.uk) and include video interviews with a wide range of experts such as social workers and mental health specialists, as well as interactive learning tools. This online resource is an evolving source of knowledge and will continue to be updated over time.

Chapter 1

Introducing the designated teacher

At a glance

- The importance of the designated teacher's role is reflected by its place in legislation and statutory guidance.
- The designated teacher's over-arching objective is to see that steps are taken to improve the educational progress and attainment of looked after children within the school.
- In acting upon this objective, the designated teacher's role can be broken down into a number of subsidiary aims, including developing and implementing the looked after child's personal education plan, and being aware of his or her wellbeing more generally.
- In order to see that the child receives the best possible support in his or her education, the designated teacher must coordinate effectively with members of staff, carers and professionals outside the school.

Introduction

> ***"I think the key quality for the designated teacher is a sense of moral purpose, that they are the person who is responsible for looked after children doing well through school, and where they have that moral purpose, it shines through."***
> Secondary school head teacher

In recent years, government has recognised the importance of taking firmer action to improve the educational attainment of looked after children and, as part of this drive, has legislated to ensure that looked after children receive strong and consistent support through the role of the designated teacher for looked after children. The Children and Young Persons Act 2008 was followed by regulation and statutory guidance to cement the position of the designated teacher and illuminate the role of the governing body in making sure he or she is supported in doing this job well. This chapter offers an overview of the role and responsibilities of the designated teacher for looked after children and sets the scene for the chapters that follow.

The role of the designated teacher is to support the looked after child's education, whatever the extra complications likely to result from the child's time in care. In doing this, all the skills and knowledge teachers normally employ within the school will be of use. But the role requires more of the designated teachers; they must always be mindful of the personal circumstances of the looked after child which may make educational achievement more difficult for them than their classmates.

At the first meeting, the looked after child is likely to see the designated teacher as just another one of the many professionals involved in their life, another adult making commitments to them, whom they may not trust. Every looked after child will have experienced some degree of separation from their parents and family and some will have had a number of care placements by the time they first come into contact with their designated teacher. For looked after children, building successful relationships with any new adult is challenging, and the designated teacher is no exception.

1.1 The role and responsibilities of the designated teacher

Key information - required qualifications for the role of designated teacher

The designated person must be:

- a qualified teacher who has completed the appropriate induction period (if required) and is working as a teacher at the school;
- a head teacher or acting head teacher of the school; or
- a member of non-teaching staff who has had responsibility for promoting the educational attainment of looked after pupils for at least six months and is taking steps to become a qualified teacher and will do so before September 2012.

The Designated Teacher (Looked After Pupils etc)(England) Regulations 2009

Being an effective designated teacher requires both a good understanding of the issues the looked after child is likely to face and an enhanced 'toolkit' of options to help support his or her learning – everything that they would do for any pupil, but also extra specialist support. It is also important to ensure the other relevant people in the looked after child's life are working for the benefit of the child's education.

Due to their being in care, looked after children will have many more professionals around them than their non-looked after peers; not merely their carers, but also their social worker, the virtual school head, the local authority's looked after children education service, mental health specialists and others. These persons form an 'extended family' around the looked after child, of which the designated teacher is an integral part. Thus, the designated teacher will find it useful to see themselves in the context of the looked after child's wider circumstances and services; their cooperation with this support network will be invaluable in ensuring the looked after child makes good educational progress.

1.2 The principal duties of the designated teacher

In anticipation of later chapters, the following points summarise the main components of the designated teacher's role:

- to work with other teachers to identify the looked after child's educational needs;
- to take lead responsibility for the child's personal education plan;
- to have high expectations for the looked after child;
- to ensure that the looked after child has access to extra learning support;
- to be aware of the wider wellbeing of the looked after child; and
- to work effectively with others, both inside and outside the school, in supporting the looked after child's learning.

Working with other teachers

In many cases, the designated teacher may not have the luxury of being forewarned that they are about to become responsible for a looked after child if, for example, the child is taken into care suddenly while they are already a current pupil at the school. In this situation, a good channel of communication with the social worker and any other relevant professionals will be important. However, in other instances, such as when a looked after child comes into school from a previous school or educational placement, it is hoped that the designated teacher will be able to liaise with the child's previous designated teacher who will be able to give a good picture of the child's learning needs and progress to date.

In either circumstance, the designated teacher should act at the earliest possible opportunity to conduct an assessment of the looked after child's educational needs, which may require an assessment of current attainment levels if that information is not already known. Particular effort should be made to ensure any assessment of special educational needs is conducted, so appropriate support can be put in place as soon as possible.

Developing and implementing the personal education plan

The personal education plan is the key resource designated teachers have for recording, planning and monitoring the looked after child's educational progress and achievement. It provides the framework around which all efforts to improve the child's educational attainment are centred. The personal education plan exists as a shared resource for all concerned with the looked after child's learning, including the looked after child themselves. It takes stock of his or her current attainment and plots a course for the future.

Each local authority will have their own specific systems and processes in place for the development and completion of the personal education plan. Whatever system is in place it is important to remember that the regulations and statutory guidance place responsibility on the designated teacher within the school for the development and implementation of the personal education plan.

Thus, the designated teacher must, with the assistance of colleagues, ensure the personal education plan is kept up to date. The initial personal education plan will be developed out of the needs assessment that occurs when the looked after child first enters care or the school. After that, the designated teacher will be responsible for taking the lead on providing content for the personal education plan. This will include: identifying ongoing educational and developmental needs, setting educational targets, recording interventions and support given, and recording academic achievement.

Having high expectations

In working with other professionals around the looked after child it is important to be conscious of the fact the previous experiences of those professionals, including teachers, may cause them to harbour negative assumptions about the capabilities of looked after children as a group. This can lead to professionals having low expectations for looked after children's educational performance. In recognition of this fact, a key tenet of outlining educational goals through the personal education plan is to ensure it sets high expectations for the child's progress, while at the same time providing all possible support to ensure the resources are in place to fulfil the educational aspirations agreed by the child and relevant professionals.

The designated teacher plays a key role in ensuring that this happens. He or she will make certain the objectives set out in the personal education plan encourage the looked after child to have confidence in their abilities, that resources are made available to broaden horizons and encourage development of new skills and interests, and will offer advice to staff and carers about the importance of holding high expectations.

Ensuring the chance to access extra learning support

Owing to a variety of factors, looked after children often fall behind their classmates in educational attainment. In the majority of these cases extra learning support has the potential to make a big difference to the progress looked after children are able to make and the designated teacher should ensure such support is provided where it will be helpful.

For example, looked after children are treated as a priority for accessing one-to-one tuition to help them catch up or reach their full potential in core subjects. The schemes available are different for each

The role of the designated teacher

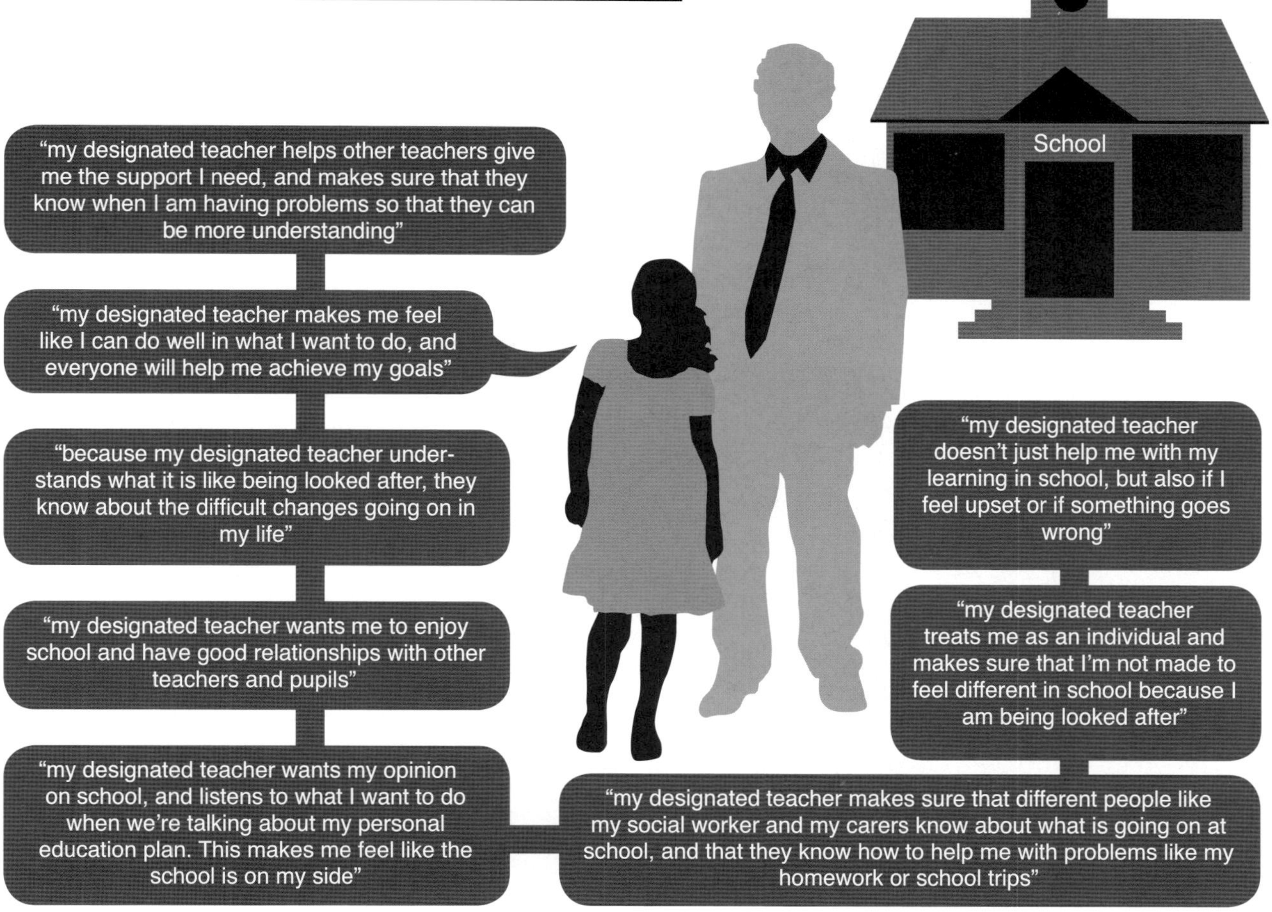

local authority. Some local authorities have specific funding available for looked after children for one-to-one tuition and home study support while others will allocate funds available to all children.

The designated teacher should determine whether extra support such as one-to-one tuition is something the child would benefit from. Although it is not always the case that one-to-one tuition is the right answer for every child who is falling behind, properly used such support can lead to significant improvements in educational attainment, particularly at KS2 and KS4. Other support provided to all children, such as homework clubs or study groups may also work well. An awareness of the different kinds of learning support available will aid the designated teacher in having an informed discussion with the looked after child about what he or she would find useful.

Being aware of the emotional, psychological and social wellbeing

Knowing key information about the child before starting work with or meeting him or her for the first time is an important initial step. The designated teacher should bear in mind that information about the child's background is not always accurately produced by the child's social worker or carer, and it may make it more difficult for the designated teacher to build a constructive relationship if his or her picture of the looked after child is mistaken. Thus, whatever advice is sought from professionals around the looked after child (or whatever information is read) it is important that the designated teacher makes sure that the child's wishes and background is taken into account. Often, interpretations of their story by others can lead to misinformation or over-sensitivity about issues that may, in reality, be quite OK with the child. It is important to remember that the child is almost always the most qualified person to tell their story and what it means for them.

This kind of information is important because it can help the designated teacher to understand the effects on the child of separation from their families, and how this is likely to impact on their success and general wellbeing at school. The designated teacher should also seek to understand what effect the personal experiences of looked after children may have on their forming strong and stable relationships with both staff members and their peers.

Looked after children frequently say that being seen as individuals by adults rather than 'in care' is very important. For each child the concerns are different: some children do not want to be treated differently by anyone in the school because they are looked after, others do not want it to appear to their peers that they are being treated differently.

In this context it is important to plan how to work with the child to avoid the feeling of being singled out, for example, when and where to meet with the child will be important. Meeting during school time, when they should be in class, may not be helpful to how they feel or to their school work. The same is true for review meetings or personal education plan reviews where having to take time out of school may make the child feel uncomfortable.

Working effectively with others inside and outside the school

The designated teacher cannot develop the personal education plan, set targets or plan support in isolation from his or her other teaching colleagues. The designated teacher's responsibility is in the oversight, planning and coordination of support for the looked after child in school – not necessarily in the delivery of that support. The child's form tutor and head of year will need to play a key role in informing this planning, agreeing targets and making commitments to the support agreed. Class teachers will be best placed to know about the child's progress and will be responsible for monitoring the day-to-day attendance, behaviour and attainment, as they would for any other child they are responsible for.

The designated teacher plays a lead role in advising and coordinating other staff within the school to ensure that the child's educational needs are met. This is likely to include informing staff of relevant developments in the personal education plan, spreading an ethos of encouragement and aspiration in which they should treat looked after children, notifying them of any parts of school policy which are tailored to looked after children, and informing them of any relevant considerations.

Outside the school, the designated teacher will ensure that he or she maintains good working relationship with both carers and professionals involved with the looked after child's learning and educational progress. The designated teacher role is also vital for ensuring that there is an initial point of contact within the school who can manage the way in which the school engages with other people involved with the learning of the looked after child. Without the carers, relevant professionals and agencies involved, it is unlikely that the personal education plan will be an effective tool in planning, monitoring and raising the educational achievement of looked after children.

In view of this, it is important to remember that the designated teacher shares the responsibility for raising the educational attainment of their looked after children with the local authority. Under the Children Act 2004 schools have a duty to cooperate with all the relevant actors across the local Children's Trust, which will include working with education, children's health and social care. The main link the designated teacher is likely to have with the local authority on a regular basis is that of the 'virtual school', through which he or she can share and receive good practice from other schools in the area, and obtain advice and support in dealing with the specific educational challenges posed by looked after children in his or her school.

Conclusion

The role of the designated teacher is an exciting one, but is a position which cannot be taken lightly. It is at once both inward and outward looking - with responsibility for ensuring the school is working to provide the looked after child with all the support he or she needs to do well, while at the same time maintaining responsibility for working in partnerships with others outside the school to provide the child with joined-up support. The role is likely to require some specialist knowledge and skills, but also a strong commitment to improving the prospects for the looked after children within the school.

What next? Further reading

- DCSF (2009). The Role and Responsibilities of the Designated Teacher for Looked After Children: Statutory Guidance for School Governing Bodies.
- DfES (2005). Common Core of Skills and Knowledge for the Children's Workforce.
- CWDC (2010). Refreshing the Common Core of Skills and Knowledge.
- Higgs, J. (2009). Corporate Parenting: The Contribution of the Designated Teacher.
- Care Matters Partnership online resources for designated teachers: www.carematterspartnership.co.uk

Chapter 2

The designated teacher, the school and the care placement

At a glance

- Looked after children are likely to have many more adults involved in their lives than their non-looked after peers.
- The designated teacher forms a crucial part of the network of people and services around the looked after child, and will need to be able to effectively communicate with these people and services to ensure that the looked after child's education is supported.
- The designated teacher should be aware of the particular role that different people and services play, and how changes in other areas of the looked after child's life may affect their educational progress and attainment.

Introduction

The designated teacher is at the centre of a team of adults, each with a role to play in supporting the looked after child. Every person involved should have the same motivation - to give the child the best possible start in life - but they will have different responsibilities, working practices and, at times, ways of communicating. Designated teachers are not expected to have the same in-depth understanding of children's social care as other professionals, but a lack of knowledge can make navigating the care system a difficult and frustrating experience.

The statutory guidance concerning designated teachers sets out clearly the expectations for liaison with other stakeholders:

Key information

"The designated teacher role is key to making sure there is a central point of initial contact – not necessarily the designated teacher him or herself – within the school who can manage the process of how the school engages with others from outside the school."[1]

DCSF (2009). The Role and Responsibilities of the Designated Teacher for Looked After Children: Statutory Guidance for School Governing Bodies

Looked after children need all the adults who play a part in their lives to work together well. Effective partnership working is not simple but its benefits for looked after children are immeasurable. Good relationships with staff within the school, and with the child's carers can help to give the looked after child consistent support, a sense of the importance of their education and a feeling of stability. This chapter provides an explanation of the role of these practitioners and guidance on how to work well with those practitioners to provide a better education for looked after children.

Key information

Designated teachers are responsible for:

- ensuring an agreed means of working with other professionals to review and develop educational attainment;

1 DCSF (2009). The Role and Responsibilities of the Designated Teacher for Looked After Children: Statutory Guidance for School Governing Bodies. Nottingham: DCSF Publications, p. 18.

- seeing that school policies are communicated to the carers, social workers and, as appropriate, the parents of looked after children;
- ensuring the child's teachers know who to contact for different reasons, e.g. in an emergency, or for signing permission slips;
- creating strong communication and partnerships between the school and relevant services, including the looked after children education service, the virtual school, and specialist services such as youth offending teams and child and adolescent mental health services.

DCSF (2009). The Role and Responsibilities of the Designated Teacher for Looked After Children: Statutory Guidance for School Governing Bodies

2.1 The designated teacher and the role of the governing body

The governing body as part of the corporate parenting structure, has responsibility for ensuring that the school is effectively safeguarding the welfare of the child and promoting his or her educational attainment. With regard to the designated teacher, they have the following statutory responsibilities:

- appointing the designated teacher;
- taking decisions about the role of the designated teacher based on the relevant information about their school. For example, if there are a large number of looked after children on the school roll, the governing body may choose to appoint more than one designated teacher, e.g one for pre-16 pupils and a second for post-16 pupils;
- deciding how best to assign the pastoral and administrative tasks of a designated teacher in the light of their own circumstances;
- providing the designated teacher with the necessary support in order to for him or her to do their job effectively. If, for example, the school has never had a looked after child on the school roll, extra support will be needed;
- liaise with the head teacher, to ensure that the designated teacher receives the appropriate training and development which is necessary for them to have up-to-date skills and knowledge and enables them to effectively respond to the teaching and learning needs of looked after children;
- liaise with the school's senior leadership team, ensuring the designated teacher contributes to a better understanding of looked after children for all relevant staff;
- the governing body should expect an annual report from the designated teacher which will allow them to make assessments of the designated teacher role and cover the key aspects of the job.[2]

What works well - Sandringham Primary School's Annual Report

Sandringham Primary School has a specific looked after children policy which defines the duties of different actors towards looked after children, including governors, designated teachers and other teaching and school staff. The head teacher and designated teacher have a responsibility to produce an annual report detailing how looked after children are doing in school. This information covers:

- the number of looked after pupils on roll (if any) and dates of joining and/or leaving;
- their attendance, as a discrete group, compared to other pupils;
- their results in their standard assessment tests, as a discreet group, compared to other pupils;
- the number and duration of fixed term and permanent exclusions (if any) as a discreet group, compared to other pupils;
- the destination of pupils who leave the school;
- the information for this report should be collected and reported in ways that preserve the anonymity and respect the confidentiality of the pupils concerned.

This report ensures that academic progress is being followed by the school and arrangements are being put in place to help looked after children thrive socially and academically, avoid exclusion or absence and ensure that adequate resources are provided for the designated teacher to support their attainment. The governing body is responsible for acting upon this information, and the annual report is shared with them, school improvement partners and Ofsted as a statutory requirement. Sandringham Primary School also provides

2 DCSF (2009). The Role and Responsibilities of the Designated Teacher for Looked After Children: Statutory Guidance for School Governing Bodies. Nottingham: DCSF Publishing, pp. 8-10.

this information to their local looked after children's education services on a termly basis, and maintains this information to ensure that joined up working is as effective as possible.

In addition to the implementation and maintenance of the statutory requirements, the governing body has a responsibility to all children, but in particular to looked after children, to ensure a positive school ethos. This involves a comprehensive implementation plan of anti-exclusion and anti-bullying policies as well as healthy living, nutrition and well-being policies. As is noted in the Every Child Matters agenda, all children and young people, including looked after children should be healthy, safe, enjoy and achieve, make a positive contribution and achieve economic well-being. The governing body is responsible for aiming to make these objectives a reality for looked after children in the school.

What next?

- Ensure that the governing body are kept up to date about the status of looked after children within the school, and agree the format for the annual report.
- Establish what training the designated teacher requires, and what provision can be made to support this.
- Liaise, where appropriate, with the governing body to ascertain the means by which other school staff are involved in raising the aspirations and attainment of looked after children.

2.2 Designated teachers and the role of the virtual school

Designated teachers should ensure that arrangements are in place within the school to facilitate effective cooperation with other professionals, especially the virtual school head (or equivalent) in the authority where their own school is located, as well as the virtual school heads from other local authorities which have looked after children on roll at the school.

DCSF (2009). The Role and Responsibilities of the Designated Teacher for Looked After Children: Statutory Guidance for School Governing Bodies

In 2007, the Department for Children Schools and Families piloted the idea of a virtual school for looked after children in ten local authorities across England. Following the widely perceived success of the pilots, in 2009 the Secretary of State for Schools, Children and Families requested that all local authorities appoint a virtual school head.

The virtual school is not, as the name might suggest, a digital, or online school. The term 'virtual' refers to the fact that it does not have a physical form; it has no school building or classes for example. The virtual school does, however, have pupils; every looked after child the local authority is responsible for or educates in a maintained school in the local authority area is part of the virtual school. It has a virtual school head, who is directly responsible for overseeing the education of looked after children in the area. This individual is usually full time and highly experienced in education with knowledge and experience of children's social care. Most virtual school heads have worked in a school as a teacher or, in some cases, as a deputy head or head teacher.

Due to the complex nature of raising educational attainment of looked after children and contributing factors outside the school's sphere of influence, it is expected that the virtual school head's position will be a senior one in the local authority. The virtual school head will report either directly to the director of children's services or to one of their deputies and have regular contact with the lead member of children's services. The virtual school head is in a position to provide unfiltered reports on the educational attainment of looked after children and provide evidence of barriers to achieving high attainment.

The virtual school head will often have a team of staff to assist them in their role. This can be one individual for a small local authority, or a team of ten or more in larger authorities. Some local authorities have kept the looked after children education services team structure with a virtual school head providing strategic oversight and a scrutiny function, others have merged the looked after children education services team into the virtual school structure reporting to the virtual school head.

For designated teachers the virtual school and virtual school head are the key points of contact with the corporate parent. They are a source of support and advice, as well as providing a service for coordinating and sharing information with other schools so as to raise the educational attainment of looked after children.

Key information - evaluation of virtual school heads pilot

- Research into virtual school heads revealed they are normally senior educationalists with a background in social work or special education. Some are employed part time.
- The size, location and function of virtual schools vary from place to place.
- Examples of good practice that virtual schools have been involved with include: a dedicated phone line for homework help and taking children from their virtual school on extracurricular trips to museums, concerts and workshops.
- Although virtual schools have direct contact with schools, teachers and pupils, the main thrust is normally one of strategy or more general awareness raising.

Berridge, D., et al. (2009). Looked After and Learning: Evaluation of the Virtual School Head Pilot.

What are the virtual school's responsibilities?

The virtual school places its focus on educational attainment and attendance for looked after children. The intention of putting in place a function and role dedicated to improving educational attainment is to redress the historical imbalance in the care system. Until now professionals involved have traditionally focused on ensuring children are safe and cared for in the best possible placements. The role of the virtual school is to ensure education is also a priority for all services and professionals around the looked after child.

Each virtual school is different, designed to meet the local authority's specific needs, however, all share common responsibilities:

- nurturing high aspirations – to set the highest aspirations for looked after children and to communicate these aspirations to all professionals around the child;
- monitoring – to track, monitor and analyse the data on educational attainment and attendance of looked after children to ensure these high aspirations are met. This data should include information on the progress of all looked after children including those who are excluded from school or not yet on a school roll and those children placed out of authority. It should be used to inform other service managers and the corporate parents (including the lead member for children's services and the director of children's services).
- responding – to respond to the data by addressing barriers to raising educational attainment and attendance at both a strategic and individual level. This includes raising awareness of specific barriers and devising strategies and initiatives to address them.
- commissioning – to plan and commission additional educational support for looked after children such as private tuition, IT equipment and other targeted initiatives such as homework clubs or extra curricular activities and learning.
- coordinating – to be a key point of coordination across all services for looked after children to ensure that all factors contributing to their educational attainment and attendance are addressed. This includes ensuring joined up working between education and children's social care professionals, as well as liaising with other authorities where children are placed out of borough and are receiving education. Virtual schools are responsible for coordinating training and support for designated teachers.

What next?

- Find out about the local authority's virtual school, its priorities for improving your school and what support it offers to designated teachers and to looked after children.
- Make contact with the virtual school head and establish a relationship. Make sure information is shared to help the virtual school head keep the looked after children database up to date. The virtual school head should keep and analyse data on the progression of children in care, their educational needs, their attendance and exclusion data, and their education, employment and training status to identify where action is needed.
- Find out what action is planned for your school, and what additional services could be provided. Think creatively about improving the attainment of the looked after children in your school.
- Find out what opportunities the virtual school provides for designated teachers to network and exchange knowledge. If there is no network in the area, suggest having one would help and determine what support the virtual school will provide to set one up.

2.3 Designated teachers and the role of the foster carer

Key information

Designated teachers should also work closely with the child's carers in any way to support educational attainment of looked after children, and the specific arrangements for each individual child should be clear to all parties involved.

DCSF (2009). The Role and Responsibilities of the Designated Teacher for Looked After Children: Statutory Guidance for School Governing Bodies

The strength of the relationship between the designated teacher and the child's carer can be the most significant factor in raising educational attainment. The more informed both parties are about the child's needs and progress in education, the more relevant and targeted the support to the looked after child.

The majority of looked after children are placed with foster carers. Fostering is a placement for a looked after child within the carer's own home. A foster care placement may comprise one adult or a couple as joint carers who sometimes have children of their own still living at home. Carers can care for more than one child at a time, if this is appropriate and there is adequate space in the home, but usually there are no more than three children at any one time.

Looked after children can stay with a foster carer for a short period of time, for example in an emergency placement or for respite care, or for a longer period of time if all parties are happy with the arrangement. Many children in foster care will at some point return to their own family although some children stay in foster care throughout their entire time in care.

What are the foster carer's responsibilities?

Foster carers are the primary source of day-to-day care for the looked after child in their care. Foster carers are required to do what every good parent would do, from welcoming them fully into their family home to supporting children to learn and develop both personally and academically in the course of their education. Foster carers support the looked after child to understand the options open to them throughout their time in care and the decisions affecting their lives. They also act as an advocate and champion for the looked after child.

Key information – foster carers' responsibilities

Leicestershire County Council have outlined foster carers' responsibilities:

1. to provide care for a foster child;
2. to promote positive health;
3. to promote a positive view of the child's family and background;

4. to promote a foster child's own race, culture and religion;
5. to promote education;
6. to let the children and young people's service know immediately of any serious incident;
7. to notify the department of any change of address;
8. to ensure the safety of any foster child whilst they are in your care;
9. to keep confidentiality;
10. to accept and ensure corporal punishment is not permitted to be used on any child placed with you;
11. to ensure that young people receive sex education appropriate to their needs;
12. to permit any person authorised by the department to see the child/young person;
13. to allow the child/young person to be removed from the foster home when so requested by a person authorised by the department;
14. to provide information to the children and young people's service and the courts if they request it, information about the child's behaviour an development.[3]

Leicester County Council. Foster Carers' Responsibilities.

The foster carer is key to supporting increased educational attainment for looked after children as they are best placed to support homework and to provide additional educational stimulation at outside school. This may be learning through play, for example, music or trips to museums. Conversely though, the foster carer's own experience of education or aspiration for the looked after child's education may be a hindrance to the child if he or she lacks of awareness of what help is needed. This point is discussed further discussed in chapter 6.

Key information - National Minimum Standards for foster carers

Standard 13: Parents' evenings, promoting educational achievement

13.1 The fostering service gives a high priority to meeting the educational needs of each child or young person in foster care and ensures that she/he is encouraged to attain her/his full potential.

The National Minimum Standards for foster carers specify that foster carers have a duty to participate in school contact in line with their placement agreement and this includes parents evenings, open days, discussions with teachers and responsibility for funding school costs such as school uniform. Foster carers must also ensure that they provide an environment whereby educational attainment is valued, and support full participation in education through home learning support. The designated teacher should be aware of the specific arrangements for each looked after child.

DoH (2002). 'Fostering Services: National Minimum Standards, Fostering Services Regulations'

What next?

- Get to know the looked after child's foster carers, make an introduction and exchange contact details.
- Put together a specific induction pack of school materials and information for carers including information about the role of the designated teacher and the personal education plan.
- Make sure the foster carer knows the child's form tutor and year head and has opportunities to attend parents' evenings, school events and awards events.
- Find out who the child's key worker is as well as the children's home manager and make contact. They will be key in supporting the child's educational progress at home.
- Liaise with the social worker to establish practicalities such as who is responsible for signing permission slips; usually this is the social worker but the responsibility can be delegated to the carer.

2.4 Designated teachers and the role of the residential home

A residential care home, often called a children's home, provides 24-hour care and trained staff as a temporary or longer-term home for looked after children. Residential care homes generally provide care for young people of secondary school age, although residents may be younger. Each child has a key worker.

3 Leicester County Council. Foster Carers' Responsibilities. Available online at: http://www.leics.gov.uk/2.1_foster_carers_responsibilities.pdf

Although most children's homes make every effort to ensure the child's transition into care is smooth and the necessary support, including counselling if they require it, is available once they are in care, challenges are likely to remain. Not least of all, looked after children often experience feelings of loneliness and/or abandonment when adapting to a new and alien environment.

The responsibilities of a children's home

The children's home must communicate with the teacher to ensure:

- they are up to date with the home-school agreement;
- there is an understanding about time-keeping and attendance;
- they are happy with any arrangements for maintaining the looked after child's homework diary;
- the child's personal education plan is on track.[4]

The designated teacher should do all he or she can to maintain an excellent working relationship with the child's carers, including working with other professionals such as the social worker in the event there is concern about the educational support the child is receiving at home.

Looked after children in residential children's homes may experience a number of challenges to their learning as a result of their home environment. The designated teacher should be sympathetic to the needs of these children and try to support their educational attainment in other ways. For example, a residential home may not have a quiet space for the child to do homework or they may be distracted by other children and find it hard to settle down. Attendance problems are often a feature of looked after children in residential settings as they may not always benefit from the kind of close care and attention present in a foster care setting, nor receive the same encouragement and impetus as fostered children.

Build strong links

It is important that the designated teacher builds a strong link with the residential carers responsible for the looked after child and ensure that they know the importance of supporting learning at home and giving each individual child time and attention to help with their homework and answer any questions they may have. It is also worth ensuring the looked after child's key worker is aware of any problems with regard to attendance and is able to support the school in addressing those. In that respect, it is important for the designated teacher to know who the key worker is for the looked after child and that communication with the key worker about the child's needs and progress is effective. This reinforces that educational attainment is important and cultivates an atmosphere in the residential home that is conducive to learning.

What next?

- Find out who the looked after child's residential carers are, establish contact and ensure both parties know how to contact each other;
- consider putting together a specific induction pack of school materials and information for carers including information about the role of the designated teacher, and the personal education plan;
- ensure the carer or key worker knows the child's form tutor and year head and has opportunities to attend parents' evenings, school events and awards events.

2.5 Designated teachers and the role of the parent

Some children who are being looked after by their local authority are in care with the full agreement of their parents, or those with parental responsibility for them such as their grandparents. These looked after children are normally in care because of particularly difficult family circumstances leading to an agreement for them to be looked after by the local authority, on a short or long-term basis. When it is

4 DCSF (2009). The Role and Responsibilities of the Designated Teacher for Looked After Children: Statutory Guidance for School Governing Bodies. Nottingham: DCSF Publications, p. 14.

the case that children are in care because of agreements with their parents or guardians, those persons retain joint parental responsibility for their children.
In other cases, however, the looked after child will be in care because of a 'care order', whereby the local authority has applied to the courts because it believes that the child is likely to suffer 'significant harm' if he or she remains with his or her family. The child's social worker will be able to give detailed information on the child's care status, should it be required.[5]

What next?

- Liaise with the social worker to clarify the role of the parent in the looked after child's school life.
- Ensure the relevant teaching and administrative staff in the school are aware of any relevant information, such as any order restricting parental access which might include collecting the child from school.

2.6 Information sharing and record keeping protocol

> ***"In my previous school some teachers talked to others about my home situation without telling me. They sometimes talked loudly to me about home in front of other pupils. I hated this."***[6]
> Year 11 pupil

Effective information sharing and multi-agency partnerships require a clear method for ensuring handling and transmitting information on looked after children. Clear mechanisms for sharing information have been laid out by the government, yet this acknowledges that all actors must use their professional judgement to decide whether to share information or not, and in what manner to do so.

This guidance is grounded in the Data Protection Act 1998, which provides a framework to ensure that personal information is handled in a 'sensible' way; to enable effective information sharing to improve services whilst maintaining safeguards and personal privacy.[7] This underpins 'the need to preserve a trusting relationship between practitioner and client with the need to share information to benefit and improve the life chances of the client or protect the public', and is based around seven specific principles for information sharing, as laid out by the government.

Seven golden rules for information sharing

By the very nature of being looked after by the local authority, a great deal of information about the child's personal life, including ongoing health needs, is documented and known to many more adults around the child than would be the case if the child was not looked after. The designated teacher will need to know and understand a significant amount of this information in order to draw up appropriate education plans with the child and other professionals, but ensuring the information is not shared inappropriately is a matter of great importance to the child. The rules around information sharing are summarised here.

In addition to knowing the rules and their importance to looked after children, there are other points about sharing information that designated teachers should keep in mind. These are points known to have tripped up other professionals in the past and are damaging to looked after children.

Firstly, when using email it is important to treat the information shared as you would in any formal communication, such as a letter or assessment report. Any information shared through email must be done so in the confidence that the person sharing it would be happy for that information to be made public. Email exchanges are subject to the legislation covered by the Freedom of Information Act.

5 DCSF (2009). The Role and Responsibilities of the Designated Teacher for Looked After Children: Statutory Guidance for School Governing Bodies. Nottingham: DCSF Publications, p. 30.
6 Ofsted (2008) Looked After Children – Good Practice in Schools. London: Ofsted, p. 9.
7 Data Protection Act 1998. London: HMSO.

Chapter 2

Secondly, be sure to avoid stating personal opinions in email exchanges with other professionals around the child and provide only professional opinion based on evidence about the child, and be aware of others failing to do this. Negative personal opinions expressed by adults responsible for supporting looked after children can be very damaging to the child's confidence and trust. The following points are taken from the Department for Children, Schools and Families' Information Sharing Pocket Guide.

Why share data?

> *"The Data Protection Act is not a barrier to sharing information but provides a framework to ensure that personal information about living persons is shared appropriately."*[8]

The designated teacher should consider why the information should be shared at all, and whether or not it is possible to gain advice on a specific issue without the need to identify the child or young person – such as not giving their name or sharing the entire case file.

Transparency

> *"Be open and honest with the person (and/or their family where appropriate) from the outset about why, what, how and with whom information will, or could be shared, and seek their agreement, unless it is unsafe or inappropriate to do so."*[9]

The designated teacher should make it clear to looked after children, their carers and other professionals that information will almost certainly need to be shared in order to provide the best support possible. However, information should be handled sensitively and efforts should be made to ensure that no information is shared beyond what is necessary, and this may mean that designated teachers should seek advice regarding specific children or young people without identifying them by name.

Seeking advice

> *"Seek advice if you are in any doubt, without disclosing the identity of the person where possible. This can help protect the designated teacher from accidentally sharing confidential information."*[10]

Confidential information is that which is private or sensitive, which means that it is "not already lawfully in the public domain or readily available from another public source; and has been provided in circumstances where the person giving the information could reasonable expect that it would not be shared with others."[11]

Share with consent

> *"Share with consent where appropriate and, where possible, respect the wishes of those who do not consent to share confidential information. You may still share information without consent if, in your judgement, that lack of consent can be overridden in the public interest."*[12]

You will need to base your judgement on the facts of the case. It would be acceptable to share information without consent if there is a risk of a child, young person or adult being put in serious harm as a consequence of not sharing the information, or if not sharing information would delay enquiries from other actors investigating cases of this nature. As such, it is generally best to gain explicit consent, verbally or in writing, from the person the information concerns. If they are not able to understand this information, such as a very young child, then consider asking whoever is responsible for them. Consent must be informed, and, as such, it should be clear what, how much and in what way this information will be shared.

8 DCSF (2008). Information Sharing Pocket Guide. Nottingham: DCSF Publications, p. 4.
9 Ibid.
10 Ibid.
11 Ibid., p. 12.
12 Ibid., p. 4.

Consider safety

> *"Consider safety and well-being: base your information sharing decisions on considerations of the safety and well-being of the person and others who may be affected by their actions."*[13]

If the designated teacher has concerns which they regard as serious enough to override a refusal of consent, they can still share this information if the safety or well-being of the person in question is threatened.

Only share when necessary

> *"Necessary, proportionate, relevant, accurate, timely and secure: ensure that the information you share is necessary for the purpose for which you are sharing it, is shared only with those people who need to have it, is accurate and up-to-date, is shared in a timely fashion, and is shared securely."*[14]

Whilst this may seem like common sense, it is important that the designated teacher differentiates between fact and opinion and only shares factually correct information with people who really need to know it. This must be done in a secure way, and the guidance recommends ensuring that information is only shared over secure e-mail or fax, or via conversations or phone calls that cannot be overheard. It is the designated teacher's responsibility to ensure that they only speak to the relevant person and confirm their identity, and ensure that if the information is going to be passed on to other actors, that the confidentiality agreements in place are upheld by these actors.

Record keeping

> *"Keep a record of your decision and the reasons for it – whether it is to share information or not. If you decide to share, then record what you have shared, with whom and for what purpose."*[15]

Regardless of whether information is shared, all records regarding looked after children should be stored securely in school and access to these files should be limited. All situations when information is shared should be recorded, however trivial, and the designated teacher should ensure that other professionals in school are sensitive to the confidentiality and rights of looked after children and young people.

2.7 Sharing information within schools

The designated teacher will need to share information with other actors both within and beyond the school on a day-to-day basis, and the majority of this information will not be subject to legal duties regarding information sharing. However, the designated teacher must be sensitive to the personal privacy of looked after children and ensure that discussions involve their input so that they feel involved and in control of their personal information.

Rules for sharing information with looked after children and young people include:

- using clear and accessible language;
- explaining there are times when confidentiality cannot be maintained.

Conclusion

This chapter has outlined the people and services that are central to improving the education of looked after children. The people discussed here serve to highlight that in helping looked after children do better the designated teacher will need the support of those who provide care at home and senior education

13 DCSF (2008). Information Sharing Pocket Guide. Nottingham: DCSF Publications, p. 4.
14 Ibid., p. 5.
15 Ibid.

specialists at the local authority. Each plays a vital part in providing support and encouragement for the looked after child, and it is vital that every one of them, including the designated teacher, cooperates effectively. This includes maintaining good channels of communication, having set procedures for information sharing, and delegating responsibility to other members of staff within the school where appropriate. Ultimately, the relationships between different people involved with the looked after child need to be understood in the context of the care system, and the child's personal care plan which provides the basis for their current and future care.

What next?

- Invest time in building relationships. Invite children and their social workers and carers in for a tour of the school and an informal meeting when the looked after child joins the school. This will establish the designated teacher as a 'friendly face' at the school that the child can turn to for support.
- Maintain contact through e-mail or phone conversations to keep in touch, and keeping a record of their contact details for emergencies.
- Ensure the child is placed firmly in the centre of any decisions taken to support them.
- Establish school procedures for sharing information and make sure all relevant staff are aware of them. .

Chapter 3

The designated teacher and other partners

At a glance

- The local authority holds responsibility for delivery against a range of important strategic duties and the designated teacher is one of many professionals with a role to play in meeting those duties.
- Elected councillors have a role to champion and advocate on behalf of looked after children, and can be a powerful ally in raising awareness of the benefit of high expectations and aspirations for looked after children.
- The social worker, independent reviewing officer and other specialist services offer vital support to looked after children in achieving well at school.

Introduction

Chapter two discussed the need for working closely with the main actors involved in the education of the looked after child. The principles that govern cooperation amongst those people and services apply equally to the range of other professionals that the designated teacher will need to coordinate with – particularly the local authority, and the child's social worker. It is important to appreciate how the individuals involved in meeting the child's wider care needs can complement his or her time in school.

A good education for the looked after child is a key component in securing his or her welfare, and is thus a primary concern of all those around the child, even if they are not specifically responsible for the looked after child's learning. As an advocate for the looked after child, the designated teacher plays an important part in communicating this message. Conversely, the designated teacher will be able to draw upon the support and expertise of the other professionals and services involved in the child's care to aid his or her education.

3.1 Designated teachers and the role of the corporate parent

> ***"We want our corporate parents to be heroes."***
> Young person on the children in care council, Walsall

Key information

Corporate parenting: the local authority has a moral and legal duty to do everything a good parent would do. These duties are specified in the Every Child Matters five outcomes.

Corporate parent: the local authority as a whole, including wider services such as health and the agencies who work on behalf of local authorities such as independent fostering providers. Ultimately the elected lead member and the director of children's services are responsible for the outcomes of looked after children.

What is a corporate parent?
For most children it is their parents who will ensure they get the best start in life. This includes keeping them safe, helping them stay healthy and happy, ensuring they access and make the best of their education, giving them opportunities to have hobbies and enjoy leisure time, and enabling them to build solid foundations for an independent and successful future.

For looked after children the local authority has this responsibility in their role as corporate parent. The term 'corporate' in this context simply refers to the collective nature of the responsibility to looked after children. Corporate parenting establishes the responsibility of the whole local authority to act as an effective parent for children within their care, directly and through partnership working with other agencies.

This 'whole authority' responsibility captures all the services and professionals that may be provided for looked after children including children's social care (social workers and care placements), education (schools and out of school education support), leisure services (access to leisure centres and other activities) and accommodation (adequate housing for care leavers). This also includes forming effective partnerships with agencies outside the direct responsibility of the local authority, including health services, child and adolescent mental health services, general practitioners, dentists, police (for looked after children who are involved in the criminal justice system) and commissioned services (fostering and residential home providers).

Agencies and professionals external to the local authority have a legal duty under the Children Act 2004 to cooperate to promote the welfare and education of children and young people in a local area, including looked after children. The body under which all the agencies are covered by this duty is known as the Children's Trust Board, a strategic partnership led by the local authority where agencies come together to agree shared priorities for all children and young people. Those agreed priorities are set out in the local children and young people's plan. Schools, health services and the police are all part of the Children's Trust Board and must work to meet the priorities set out in the plan.

Elected members (councillors) have a collective responsibility to ensure looked after children get the support and services they need to get the best start in life. The principal responsibility falls onto the lead member for children's services and the director of children's services.

At an operational level many people and agencies are involved in ensuring this happens. These include senior officers and managers in the local authority, frontline staff such as social workers, carers, teachers and education support staff, and others from specialist services such as mental health professionals.

What are the corporate parent's responsibilities?
Being a good corporate parent means the organisations, services and individuals involved should be working to provide the care and support that any good parent would for their own children.

To focus this overarching aim, in 2008 the Department for Children, Schools and Families revised the five outcomes for looked after children first introduced under the Every Child Matters agenda in 2004. These outcomes provide the framework for corporate parents' responsibilities to looked after children, taking into account their individual needs, wishes and feelings. They state looked after children should: be healthy, stay safe, enjoy and achieve, make a positive contribution and achieve economic well-being. A full list of the aspects of these outcomes can be found in appendix I.

The Children Act 2004 places a duty on corporate parents to promote the educational attainment of looked after children. Schools have a duty to proactively work with the local authority to achieve this.

Key information - Four important duties for local authorities

In regard to looked after children's educational achievement, local authorities must ensure that:

- looked after children have educational outcomes comparable to their peers;
- all local authority processes demonstrate a proactive commitment to educational outcomes for looked after children;
- all looked after children are encouraged to have high expectations;
- there is sufficient training and support for all local authority staff to facilitate understanding of the needs of looked after children.

DfES (2005). Statutory Guidance: Duty on Local Authorities to Promote the Educational Achievement of Looked After Children

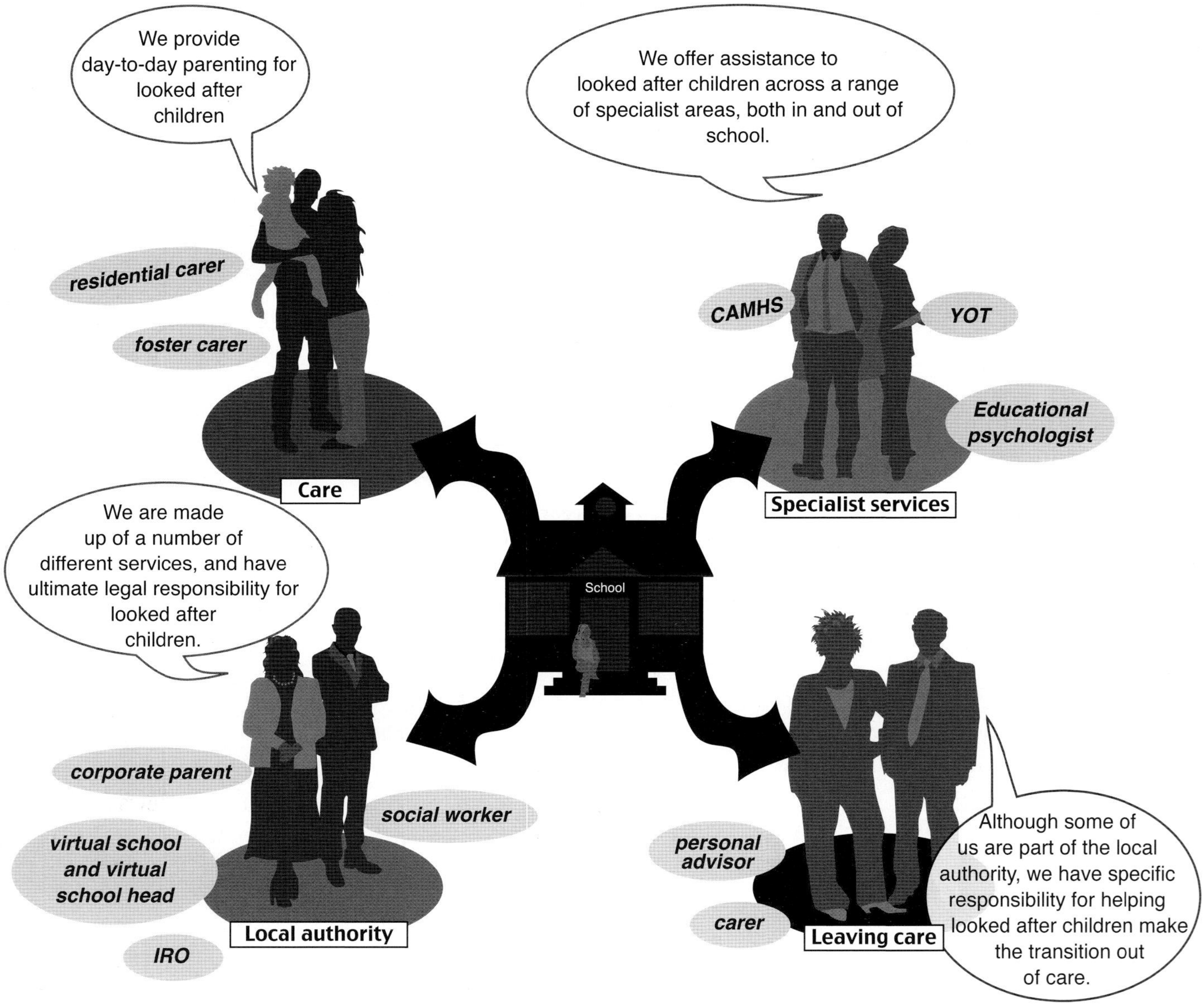

How is corporate parenting structured and monitored?

The Government has mechanisms to ensure corporate parents meet their responsibilities under the Every Child Matters framework. This is done in the ways listed below.

Transparency in outcomes reporting

Local authorities are required to report on performance against a number of national indicators. These are a group of targets against which all local authorities are measured. The performance of the local authorities and their children's trust partners are measured against the following indicators on the outcomes for children and young people, with a number of indicators specific for looked after children. These include the following:

- **NI 73:** Achievement at level four or above in both English and maths at key stage 2;
- **NI 75:** Achievement of five or more A*- C grades at GCSE or equivalent including English and maths;
- **NI 76:** Reduction in number of schools where fewer than 55% of pupils achieve level four or above in both english and maths at KS2;
- **NI 84:** Achievement of two or more A*- C grades in Science GCSEs or equivalent;
- **NI 117:** 16 to 18 year olds who are not in education, employment or training.

A full list can be found in Appendix II

Inspection and regulation
Local authorities and children's services are subject to regular inspection, something that designated teachers will have some experience of with school Ofsted inspections. Similar to school inspections, Ofsted will inspect the services provided to looked after children by looking in detail at the organisation (leadership and governance) and at the operations (workforce, standards and services).

Most importantly for designated teachers, Ofsted will look at the 'enjoy and achieve' progress and the arrangements put in place by the local authority to raise educational attainment for looked after children. This will often include talking to children and young people as well as looking at the effectiveness of the role of the designated teacher within the school.

Independent advocacy and complaints
Under Article 12 of the United Nations Convention on the Rights of the Child and the Children Act 1989, looked after children have a right to advocacy and to have their opinions listened to. On behalf of looked after children advocates provide a mixture of representation, support, empowerment and protection of rights. Advocates are usually professionally trained in social or youth work, education, childcare or law and have experience of working with children and young people.
All looked after children and care leavers have the right to be represented in making complaints about decisions that affect them. Many local authorities employ a Children's Rights Officer to assist with a child's right to advocacy, ensuring the looked after child or care leaver has access to the advocacy services he or she is entitled to.

The Children's Rights Director for England, currently Dr Roger Morgan, is part of the national standards and regulation framework and exists to ask looked after children and care leavers for their views about the care they receive. The Children's Rights Director publishes the views of looked after children and care leavers using the information they have to give advice on how the Government could provide more effective care and support.

The children's pledge
All local authorities must have a children's pledge for looked after children. The pledge is a set of promises the local authority as corporate parent makes to looked after children and care leavers about the care and support they will receive. It should be highly inspirational for looked after children and be developed taking into account their views, wishes and feelings. The pledge should also state what looked after children can expect from the local authority, as their corporate parent, and how the corporate parent intends to make sure promises are fulfilled. Pledges might include not moving looked after children if they are happy in their current placement, or making sure they have internet access at home. The authority should ensure looked after children are aware of the pledge.

What works well

Redcar & Cleveland Borough Council set up a task force involving their children in care to develop their children's pledge. The final version made seven promises to the children:

- to listen and respect the child;
- to provide good services such as a designated teacher;
- to look after the health of the child;
- to keep the child safe;
- to secure for the child the best education;
- to involve the child in interesting activities;
- to achieve economic wellbeing.

All looked after children in Redcar and Cleveland have a copy of the pledge which they discuss with those caring for them. There is an annual review of the pledge's success and children in the care council are given the opportunity to raise any issues about it with the corporate parenting board.

What next?

Think about using the children's pledge to put together a school pledge for looked after children. This would set out how the school will ensure the relevant aspects of the children's pledge will be met. A copy could be provided to any looked after children enrolling in the school and any professional involved in their life so that the school might be held accountable to its promises. This would assist in developing a 'whole school approach' to looked after children.

The children and young people's plan

If the children's pledge sets out the vision for services to looked after children then the children and young people's plan specifies how this vision will be achieved. The children and young people plan is the strategic plan for all aspects of services to children and young people; it sets out the duty of all partner agencies to cooperate. The plan must address looked after children as a specific priority group and provide benchmarks and targets as well as strategic priorities to ensure these targets are met. The educational attainment and attendance of looked after children are prioritised within all children and young people's plans.

Elected members are informed and engaged

Although it is the lead member for children's services who is politically accountable for looked after children, all elected members are corporate parents. Elected members mostly come from non-social care professional backgrounds and induction and training to be a corporate parent should be offered by the local authority. Elected members are not involved in operational activity, but set the strategic direction of services and arrange resources to support their delivery and implementation.

Many local authorities also have some form of corporate parenting panel or board which monitors key performance indicators and address the strategic policy issues that have an impact on looked after children. Each local authority has their own way of doing this and some panels include unelected members such as senior managers, officers, foster carers or head teachers. Educational attainment and attendance is a key issue they monitor.

What next?

Some corporate parenting panels have frontline staff represented either as members of the panel or to give presentations about their work. It is rare to have a designated teacher as a member of a panel but this could be an interesting idea to propose to the local authority, particularly if the designated teacher is also the head teacher. Using frontline experience to inform policy at corporate parenting level can be a powerful means to improve services for looked after children.

All schools will have at least one elected member on their school governing body. Keeping them informed about the school's work, as well as about any local authority policy barriers having a negative impact in raising attainment and attendance for looked after children, may provide a useful means to removing these barriers. It is best to do this with the support and knowledge of the head teacher.

The children in care council

Local authorities are expected to establish a children in care council to ensure looked after children have their views heard and enable them to participate in decision making about the services provided to them. Each children in care council will be structured differently to suit the needs of the local authority and its looked after children. The children in care council is expected to engage with all looked after children including: those who are hard to engage, those in and out of authority placements, younger children, those with disabilities or special needs and unaccompanied asylum seeking children.

The children in care council is a powerful mechanism for looked after children to hold corporate parents to account for their commitments under Every Child Matters outcomes and the local authorities children's pledge. Most children in care councils have a link to the corporate parenting panel, the director of children's services and the lead member as well as other service managers.

For designated teachers, the children in care council can provide useful strategic feedback from looked after children about the services and support they receive to raise their educational attainment. It is a useful means of benchmarking the local authority's expectations for looked after children in education against the children's individual and collective experiences.

What next?

- Find out about the local authority's children in care council and ask for some information on how looked after children can get involved. Consider how best to encourage and support the looked after children in this. Participation of this kind can help children develop confidence, teamwork skills and have a positive impact on their behaviour in school as well as their approach to and passion for learning.
- Think about how to engage looked after children in the school's mechanisms for participation such as the school council. This has individual benefits of allowing the looked after child to feel more a part of the school, build positive relationships within his or her peer group. Involvement can also serve to promote positive images of looked after children across the school.

3.2 Designated teachers and the role of the social worker

All looked after children will have a social worker. The social worker will assess the individual needs of the child, taking into account the child's views as well as those of specialist professionals, and use their professional judgement to respond to those needs. Social workers are trained professionals, with a graduate or post-graduate level qualifications. They will have knowledge of the laws relevant to children, particularly in terms of child protection, and are often responsible for working with legal professionals in the local authority to make representations to the courts to keep children safe. They have extensive statutory powers and responsibilities, under the Children Acts of 1989 and 2004, and the Children and Young Person's Act 2008. In addition to their statutory powers and responsibilities, social workers also have professional standards and regulatory bodies which monitor these standards nationally.

Key information - the social worker

Role includes:

- helping to secure the wellbeing of children, adults, families and communities;
- enabling every child and young person to fulfil their potential, including achieving independence;
- being supportive and considerate;
- a commitment to the worth, dignity and individuality of each person;
- ability to work well with colleagues and other professionals;
- ability to work in high-pressure situations in situations that are complex, stressful and risk; and
- knowledge and understanding of the locality in which they work and awareness of the available resources.

General Social Care Council (2008). Social Work at its Best: A Statement of Social Work Roles and Tasks for the 21st Century

What are the social worker's responsibilities?

Social workers are responsible for planning support for the looked after child through the care plan and liaising with the relevant professionals and services needed to implement the care plan. The social worker also plays a key pastoral role - getting to know the child and understanding what their views, feelings and wishes are. Listening to the child and being responsive to what they want is a big part of this, and although since actions will not always reflect the child's wishes exactly, clear explanations should be given. Good social workers will sometimes need to challenge other professionals' decisions about the child's life to ensure the best possible opportunities are made available.

Given the social worker is responsible for planning the child's care and support, he or she will have a primary interest in the child's education, as part of their responsibility for the child's overall care. The social worker is the individual who organises reviews, contact visits with birth parents and access to specialist services such as therapists. The social worker is also responsible for making sure that children have a school place and that they have all the support needed to achieve in their education. Designated teachers need to know who a looked after child's social worker is and to liaise with them.

What next?

- Get to know the social workers responsible for the care plan of the looked after children in the school.
- Keep a list of contact details including emergency numbers.
- Arrange to meet the social worker to gain information on the details of the care plan and to discuss the school's arrangements to improve the educational attainment of looked after children.

3.3 Designated teachers and the role of the independent reviewing officer

The role of the independent reviewing officer is a crucial component in the framework for assessing whether or not the local authority and the professionals working for that authority are fulfilling their legal duties in respect to the looked after child. This will be done primarily through the independent reviewing officer's role as chair of the review meetings, where they will seek to ascertain how effective the care plan is and establish the extent to which the appropriate goals are being met.

The independent reviewing officer is likely to have regular contact with the designated teacher, depending upon the particular circumstances of the looked after child, but will also work closely with children's service teams and will provide reports on the quality of care planning. In cases where the independent reviewing officer feels care planning is poor, they will take action to notify the local authority before deciding whether or not to pursue action through informal or formal channels.

What are the independent reviewing officer's responsibilities?

The local authority responsible for the looked after child is required to appoint an independent reviewing officer to carry out the following functions:

- to participate in the review of the looked after child's overall care plan ('the case review');
- to monitor the performance of the local authority when reviewing the child's case, in particular to check they are fulfilling their legal duty of care to the looked after child;
- to take the appropriate steps after assessing the local authority's performance, including referring the case to the Children and Family Court Advisor and Support Service.

Who supports children and young people with mental health problems?

Child and adolescent mental health services (CAMHS) comprise a number of different professionals from different disciplines, working in teams to support children and young people with complex mental health needs. Some areas have a specialised child and adolescent mental health services looked after children team that provides services explicitly for looked after children in one place, whilst in others this will be part of general child and adolescent mental health services. As mental health needs are much more common amongst looked after children, these services can offer specialised support.[1]

[1] Royal College of Psychiatrists (2004). Child Abuse and Neglect: the Emotional Effects. Factsheet for Parents and Teachers. Mental Health and Growing Up, Factsheet 19. London: Royal College of Psychiatrists.

What next?

- Understand the care planning and review process.
- Ensure that the appropriate arrangements are set up with the social worker to provide notification of any changes to the care plan which will affect or disrupt the looked after child's education.

3.4 Designated teachers and the role of leaving care services

Key information

"The designated teacher should... promote a culture in which looked after children believe they can succeed and aspire to further and higher education."

DCSF (2009). The Role and Responsibilities of the Designated Teacher for Looked After Children – Statutory Guidance for School Governing Bodies

There are a range of private and public facilities on offer for young people when making the transition out of care, which are grouped under the generic label of 'leaving care services'. Examples include information, advice and guidance services (e.g. Connexions careers service), counselling services, youth justice and legal advocacy groups, and housing services. Looked after children may draw upon the knowledge of various professionals including their social worker and designated teacher, but the most important person will be the personal advisor from the leaving care team, who mentors the young person into the post-care world. Together with the social worker and the looked after child, personal advisors are responsible for formulating a 'pathway plan', which replaces the care plan once the young person reaches 16. The pathway plan will assess the child's needs, and make arrangements for their education, accommodation, employment and other needs once they leave care.

The personal advisor

The personal advisor will liaise with the relevant services to ensure:

- the looked after child receives advice (including practical advice) and support in leaving care;
- the looked after child has an effective working plan for leaving care (the pathway plan);
- the personal advisor and other relevant professionals are involved in reviewing the pathway plan;
- there is coordinated provision of services, and reasonable steps are taken to ensure the young person makes use of such services;
- the personal advisor keeps in touch with looked after children and care leavers up to the age of 21, or beyond if they are on an approved programme of education or training.

What works well – volunteer support to pathway planning in Gateshead

The leaving care team in Gateshead provides support to around 150 young people leaving care every year. For those over 18s who have been looked after, a support worker is offered to assist in getting that young person started in life.

In addition to this, the services of a volunteer mentor are offered, which would be written into the young person's pathway plan.
All volunteers are trained by the leaving care team and can encourage them to consider a volunteer mentor when they are working on the pathway plan with a young person, to go alongside the expected services such as help with accommodation, practical skills, education and training, employment, and financial support.

Independent living

Living independently is one option for looked after children over the age of 16; 42% of all care leavers are living in this way by age 19.[2] Whilst independent living has a number of benefits and can raise self-esteem, it does confer a lot of responsibility on to the young person and this can be particularly challenging for those still in full time education. They must develop the emotional resilience and practical self care skills necessary to look after themselves, alongside managing their own education which would otherwise be supported by parents or carers in other circumstances. This would include

2 NCAS (2009). Journeys to Home: Care leavers' successful transition to independent accommodation. London: National Care Advisory Service, p. 49.

help with homework, praise and motivation, help with time management, emotional support during stressful periods such as exams, careers guidance and support with making decisions about the future. Looked after children or care leavers living independently may feel lonely and find it difficult to manage their learning independently. The designated teacher can help support the young person's educational attainment by discussing the difficulties raised by independent living and including these considerations in the personal education plan, work with other actors and in the pastoral support the child receives.

This may include using afterschool study groups if the young person finds it hard to concentrate at home, or support arranging extra tuition or answering questions they may have quickly and easily. They will require additional support in making decisions about the future, planning for revision and exams; and the designated teacher can help them to organise their learning (such as designing a revision timetable) or gain further advice from other services such as careers advisors. In many areas the leaving care team can provide practical support for transitions in to independent living such as 'training flats' with support and self care skills training which the designated teacher can arrange.

What next?

- Ensure that the looked after child has access to all the relevant information about further education and careers guidance.
- Make time to discuss the possibilities for the young person once they leave year 11.
- Be aware of the child's living situation and offer appropriate support; and as part of the personal education plan, discuss what activities or study support can be used to bolster aspirations for further education and allow the young person to broaden their horizons.

3.5 The designated teacher and the role of specialist services

Key information

"Some [looked after children] require the involvement of other professionals,
for example, SEN and CAMHS services...The designated teacher role is key to making sure there is a central point of initial contact – not necessarily the designated teacher him or herself – within the school who can manage the process of how the school engages with others from outside of the school."

DCSF (2009). The Role and Responsibilities of the Designated Teacher for Looked After Children – Statutory Guidance for School Governing Bodies

Aside from the leaving care teams mentioned above, there are a number of other specialist services which the looked after child may benefit from using. In particular, child and adolescent mental health services within the local health authority are likely to offer a range of services that are applicable to looked after children. Some areas even offer a specialist looked after children unit within their mental health services, which offers tailored advice and mental health support.

Aside from child and adolescent mental health services, there are a number of other specialist services that may be of use in supporting looked after children, including:

- school nursing services;
- housing officers;
- looked after children's nurses;
- stay safe services;
- voluntary services and charities (e.g. the Police Cadets, the Duke of Edinburgh Award, the Princes' Trust);
- youth offending teams;
- educational psychologists.

Any such support will be coordinated through the social worker and recorded in the care plan. The designated teacher should be able to use his or her expertise of the educational needs of the child to make recommendations as to any extra support that the looked after child might receive to help him or her in school.

What next?

- Understand the different services and what they can offer the looked after child.
- Establish arrangements with the child's social worker for flagging up arrangements for suggesting the intervention of specialist services.

3.6 The importance of working together

The designated teacher is the first point of contact for any issues regarding the education of looked after children, both within the school and in many areas beyond it. This responsibility includes working with other teachers and staff within the school, other service providers, the children or young people themselves, carers and families. As these relationships reflect very different aspects of the looked after child's life and require different levels of interaction, they will require different skills and methods of communication.

Key information

Schools will increasingly need to operate within a local system of schools and service providers, including the Children's Trust within which are a statutory 'relevant partner'. This will mean schools, and specialist staff such as designated teachers, working closer with other schools and other service providers, including health and children's social care. By working in this way, schools can share expertise, take early and preventative action and commission services that improve well-being for all their pupils and children in the locality, including the most vulnerable.

DCSF (2009).The Role and Responsibilities of the Designated Teacher for Looked After Children: Statutory Guidance for School Governing Bodies.

Multi-agency working is crucial for providing all round services for looked after children and the designated teacher will need to build effective relationships with the different actors involved in the looked after child's life. This ensures that the support looked after children receive is consistent and result in arrangements that are important to the looked after child, such as minimising school moves at important times, or ensuring that the child or young person's care review considers all aspects of their wider situation. The designated teacher will need to communicate with different actors in order to understand and respond to different needs. This will involve:

- direct and frequent involvement with carers, social workers and parents (where relevant) to ensure day-to-day support for education outside school hours;
- ongoing communication with other teachers and other professionals responsible for supporting the attainment of looked after children, such as subject and form teachers, the virtual school head, looked after children education services teams, special educational needs coordinators, child and adolescent mental health services and leaving care teams as appropriate;
- consistent participation in the child's care review, and communication with the independent reviewing officer so that the needs of the personal education plan are taken in to account; and
- potential involvement in promoting the interests of looked after children to the Children's Trust Board, allowing actors to influence higher level decision making and share best practice in supporting looked after children and advocating for their needs.[3]

These relationships are all very important and serve to satisfy the different needs of looked after children, from signing permission slips for school trips to improving how services for looked after children are run. The designated teacher will need to develop a close relationship with the virtual school head and

3 DCSF (2009). The Role and Responsibilities of the Designated Teacher for Looked After Children: Statutory Guidance for School Governing Bodies. Nottingham: DCSF Publications, p. 18.

looked after children education services team for their area who ensure the educational needs of all looked after children in the authority are met, they may also work with virtual school heads from other authorities which have looked after children on their school rolls.

The statutory guidance lays out the arrangements that should be in place for communication and multi-agency partnership, in that:

- there is an agreed process in place for how the school works in partnership with other professionals, such as the child's social worker and the child's carer, in order to review and develop the child's educational progress and how each person will contribute to driving up the child's educational achievement;
- school policies in relation to, for example, home-school agreements, time-keeping and attendance, homework diaries and parents' evenings are communicated to carers and social workers and, where appropriate, birth parents, so that looked after children are not disadvantaged;
- the child's teachers know the most appropriate person to contact where necessary. For example, in some cases authority to sign permission slips for school trips will be delegated to the foster carer but for some children permission will be needed from the child's social worker;
- there are positive and effective channels of communication and partnership working between the school and relevant partners to help looked after children get the most out of their school experience. This may result in the need to work with professionals from local authorities, such as virtual school heads, and dedicated looked after children education teams, special educational and child and adolescent mental health services.[4]

Ensuring effective communication can be difficult when handling a number of different relationships, but it is important that its value in providing effective support for looked after children is recognised. The designated teacher's primary means of facilitating this is by maintaining an up to date personal education plan that accurately reflects the attainment and needs of the looked after child, so that it can be used by other practitioners and as a timely and relevant part of the care plan.

The value of effective communication is also reflected in the designated teacher's role as a source of information and consultation for any developments or decisions that will affect the looked after child's education - including potential exclusions - so that they can advocate for the child, minimise disruption and ensure smooth transitions where changes are unavoidable. In this instance he or she has a duty to communicate all relevant information to the new school and local authority, and ensure that the child is involved in these processes and has their voice heard.

Key information - The Gatsby Project, Derby

The Gatsby Project was set up to measure the success of the designated teacher role, in the context of multi-agency efforts to support looked after children and young people across the local authority. Overall, it found that designated teachers were aware of the "multi-dimensional nature of the role, with their work involving liaison with other professionals and carers, advocacy for the looked after child, maintaining an overview of children's progress and ensuring personal education plans were undertaken".[5] Below is a summary.

Within school

- "Contact was somewhat problem-focused and often concerned with behavioural issues, rather than generally getting to know the children or find out about their learning experience", with pastoral care provided by class teachers, tutors or heads of year, and a strong whole school approach.[6] Some looked after children were not aware of who their designated teacher was or what they could offer. Direct contact would sometimes occur but it "could not be assumed or expected that such a positive relationship would be possible".[7]

4 DCSF (2009). The Role and Responsibilities of the Designated Teacher for Looked After Children: Statutory Guidance for School Governing Bodies. Nottingham: DCSF Publications, p. 18.
5 Fletcher-Campbell, F., Archer, T., and Tomlinson, K. (2004). The Role of the School in Supporting the Education of Children in Public Care. Nottingham: DfES Publications, p. 4.
6 Brodie, I., Berridge, D., Dobel-Ober, D., and Sinclair, R., (2006). Taking Care of Education. Final Report to the Gatsby Charitable Foundation. London: National Children's Bureau, p. 7.
7 Ibid, p10

- The personal education plan review meeting was regarded as an important time for meeting with social workers and carers, sharing information and an opportunity to focus attention on education issues, but the purpose and value of the personal education plan itself was regarded as debatable and seen as unimportant by some actors and children – including being seen as 'just another piece of paper'.
- The designated teacher was seen as an important connection between the looked after child's care and education experiences.

The designated teacher's view

- Designated teachers saw multi-agency working as a key part of their role, maintaining strong relationships and regular contact. Communication focused on:
- strategies for support;
- crisis management;
- formal review; and
- planning meetings.
- Significant problems included communication over key information such as looked after children's circumstances, changes in placement or social worker and organising meetings – with formal complaints being made by several designated teachers regarding timeliness and quality of information sharing from social services, this was seen as a lack of continuity and sensitivity towards looked after children.
- designated teachers often found it difficult to get information from social services, other schools and education departments – such as the passing along of personal education plans when school placements moved.
- Information sharing and confidentiality were concerns for looked after children, and there was great variation in how such concerns were addressed by different designated teachers. Whilst information sharing was seen as necessary, there was no common understanding or guidance on how to do this. Concerns included:
- fear of stigmatising looked after children;
- wanting to maintain equal opportunities; and
- lack of consultation with looked after children themselves.

What next?

- Establish links with the practitioners responsible for different looked after children on the school roll, such as social workers. Not only will they have a deeper understanding of the looked after children they are responsible for, they have extensive knowledge and practical skills for working with looked after children and may be able to support the designated teacher in developing their own abilities.
- Developing a 'united front' of practitioners all working with the same looked after child or young person and having close communicative relationships is the most effective way of ensuring cohesive, mutually supportive services.

Conclusion

This chapter has outlined some of the significant people and services that are involved in the lives of looked after children. Each plays a vital part in providing support and encouragement for the looked after child, and it is vital that every one of them - including the designated teacher - coordinates effectively. This includes maintaining good channels of communication, having set procedures for information sharing, and delegating responsibility to other members of staff within the school where appropriate. Ultimately, the relationships between different people involved with the looked after child need to be understood in the context of the care system, and the child's personal care plan which provides the basis for their current and future care. This is discussed in the next chapter.

What next? Further reading

- DCSF (2010). Promoting the Educational Achievement of Looked After Children: Statutory Guidance for Local Authorities.
- DCSF (2010). IRO Handbook.
- DCSF (2009). Care Matters: Ministerial Stocktake Report.
- Care Matters Partnership online resources for designated teachers: www.carematterssparnership.co.uk

Chapter 4

Introducing the care system

At a glance

- The care system is a complex set of services that has undergone significant changes in recent decades, particularly since 2000.
- There are a number of key pieces of legislation that underpin the care system which the designated teacher should be aware of. These include the Children Act 1989, the Children Act 2004, and the Children and Young Persons Act 2008.
- Children come into care for a variety of reasons, and the nature of their care experience will depend upon both their background experiences and the different types of care setting into which they are placed.
- The child's care plan is the central document in his or her progression through care. It includes information on the looked after child's health, education, protection and placement, and is reviewed regularly to ensure that the child's needs are being met.

Introduction

This chapter provides an overview of the care system, setting out its history and providing an explanation of the key legislative provisions. Understanding the system in this way allows designated teachers to picture the context in which education is provided to looked after children, and sets out the legal basis which underpins local authorities' duties to care for and accommodate looked after children. The chapter illustrates the needs of looked after children through statistical analysis and describes how care and accommodation are provided. This information will serve as a helpful background for designated teachers, helping them discharge their duties as effectively as possible.

4.1 The legal foundations of the care system

The care system in something like its present form has been around since at least 1948, when the then government introduced legislation to act upon the recommendations of the Curtis Report (1946). Unfortunately, then, as today, the legislation regarding children in care was often pre-empted by scandals involving the treatment of children.[1] In the case of the Curtis Report, the immediate motivation was the death in foster care of Dennis O'Neill, who was found starved and beaten. The resulting Children Act 1948 set up children's departments in every local authority, which were made responsible for overseeing the care of all looked after children.[2]

In the years that followed legislation on looked after children was relatively sparse, with notable exceptions including the Children and Young Persons Act 1963. Giving local authorities the power to provide funding to keep children and young people out of care, and the Children Act 1975, which made provisions to facilitate easier adoption.[3] However, in 1984 the House of Commons social services select

1 See Jackson, S. (2006). Looking After Children Away From Home: Past and Present, in Chase, Simon and Jackson (eds.) In Care and After: a Positive Perspective. Abingdon: Routledge.

2 House of Commons, Children, Schools and Families Committee (2009). Looked-after Children: Third Report of Session 2008-9, Volume 1. London: The Stationery Office.

3 Ibid., p. 23.

committee published a report on the status of the care system, in which the committee noted a number of systemic weaknesses, including not providing enough support for families, failing to sufficiently take into account the views of parents or young people, and failure to tackle the poor outcomes of care leavers.[4] The subsequent Children Act 1989, remains a core piece of legislation.

Since 1997 there has been extra funding and expertise provided via the dual Quality Protects (1998) and Choice Protects (2002) initiatives, which introduced the notion of local authorities as corporate parents and instigated measures to deal with the poor outcomes of looked after children. However, despite the extra resources, outcomes for looked after children remained poor relative to those of their non-looked after peers. These perceived deficiencies in tackling the challenges faced by looked after children are reflected in the current Care Matters programme, which was set in motion in 2006. Suggesting wide-ranging and ambitious reform, much of the Care Matters programme's policy recommendations - including the new role of designated teacher for looked after children – became statute in the Children and Young Person's Act 2008.

The key acts underpinning the care system

Children Act 1989

The Children Act 1989 remains a foundational piece of legislation, which still provides the most general legal basis for looked after children. Most subsequent legislation has either amended or supplemented sections of the act, although large parts of it remain relevant. Its key provisions in regard to looked after children are that local authorities must:

- safeguard and promote the welfare of all looked after children [sec. 22(3)(a)];
- consult the looked after child and give proper consideration to his or her race, culture, religion and linguistic background before making any decisions [sec. 22(4)-(5)];
- accommodate each looked after child and provide whatever else, apart from accommodation, is need to support them; [sec. 23(1)]
- advise, assist and befriend the looked after child with respect to promoting his or her welfare after they cease to be looked after; [sec. 24A];
- carry out the relevant duties in co-operation with other agencies, i.e. as a 'corporate parent' [sec. 27].

The Children Act 1989 provides the legal basis under which children and young people are taken into care:

Section 20 – Under this section, a child is taken in to care through voluntary agreement with his or her parents. This section also states that the child cannot be taken into care if those persons with parental responsibility object to that happening. In both cases, the parents are only eligible if either (i) they are willing and able to provide accommodation for the child, or (ii) they are willing and able to arrange that accommodation is provided.[5] Parents of children in care under section 20 will continue to have a strong say in decisions about the child's care.

Section 31 – known as a 'care order', a child is taken into care under section 31 when a local authority or other relevant person applies to a court to have the child put under their supervision. The court will only grant the care order if the child is suffering or likely to suffer from significant harm and only if that (prospective) harm is a result of either (i) the sub-standard of care from the child's parents, or (ii) the child being beyond parental control.[6]

Section 44 – A child is typically taken into care under section 44 of the Children Act 1989 if there is reasonable cause to believe that he or she is likely to suffer significant harm if urgent action is not taken. This is known as an 'emergency protection order' and might include circumstances in which the child is suffering, or likely to suffer physical or sexual abuse.[7]

4 Social Services Committee, Second Report of Session 1983–84, Children in care, HC 360.
5 The Children Act 1989, section 20(7).
6 The Children Act 1989, section 31(1;2).
7 The Children Act 1989, section 44(1).

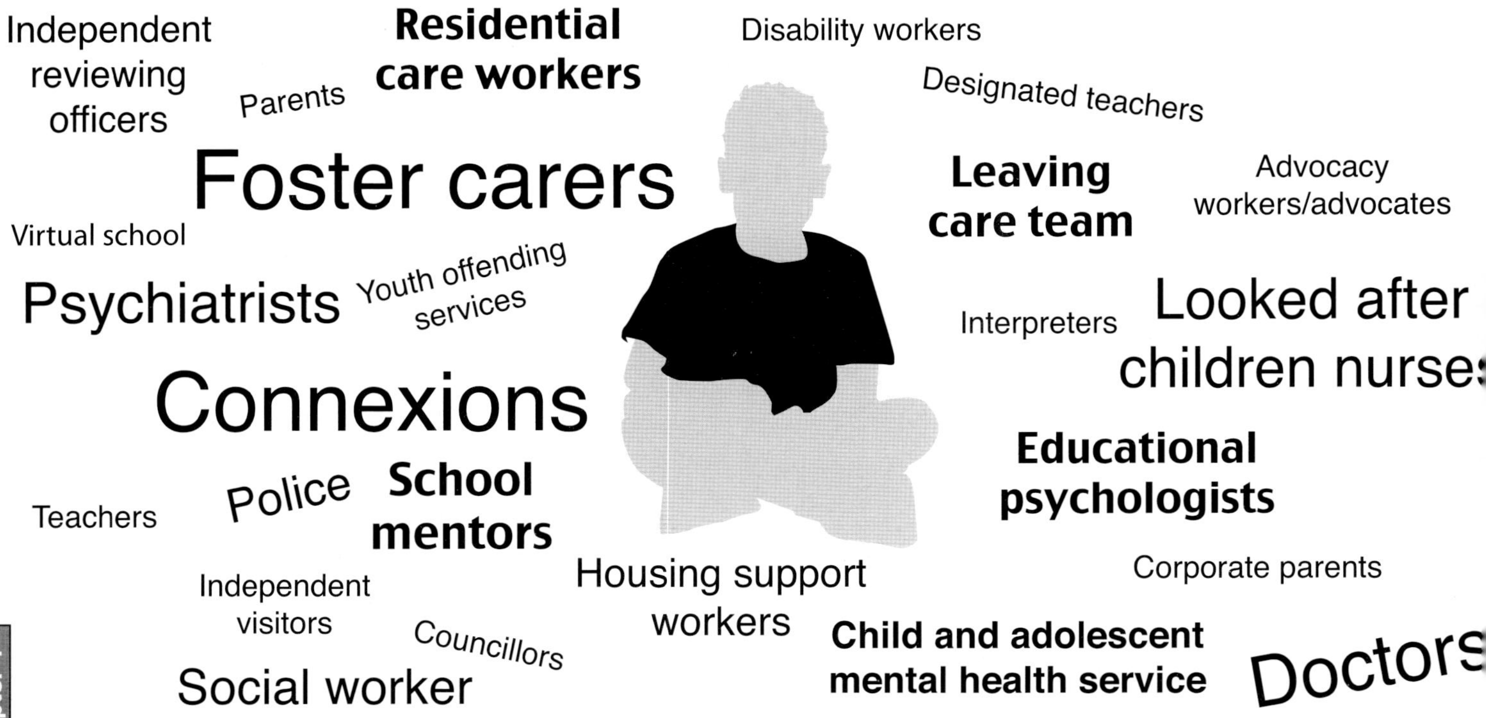

<u>Care Standards Act 2000</u>

The Care Standards Act 2000 made a number of changes to how the care system is regulated, including those cases where care is provided by private and voluntary services, in order to provide stronger quality assurance. Most importantly, the act:

- established independent regulation of care services, including children's homes but also nursing homes and independent hospitals [sec. 23];
- set out rules regarding the regular inspection of these services [sec. 31];
- established independent bodies to register social workers and set standards for their education and training [part IV].

<u>Children (Leaving Care) Act 2000</u>

The Children (Leaving Care) Act 2000 is designed to improve outcomes for care leavers. It makes a number of important changes to the law, including conferring legal duties to local authorities which had previously been discretionary. Local authorities must:

- discharge their differential duties in regard to the three new groups of young people ('eligible', 'relevant' and 'former relevant') created by the act in regard to age, length of time in care, and care status (for definitions, see the glossary);
- provide all children and young people in care with a 'needs assessment' detailing his or her post-care requirements, and a resulting 'pathway plan' which outlines how these needs are to be met;
- provide all children or young people in care or care leavers with a 'personal advisor' to oversee the implementation of the pathway plan;
- provide other assistance (such as financial support or accommodation) in meeting the goals set out in the pathway plan.

<u>Children Act 2004</u>

The Children Act 2004 makes further provision for 'joining up' various national and local services dealing with children and young people. In particular, the act:

- creates the post of Children's Commissioner for England, with responsibility for promoting the views of children and young people, including those that are looked after [sec. 1];
- places the relevant services (e.g. local authorities, schools, the police, Primary Care Trusts) under a duty to co-operate in working to protect children [sec. 10];
- gives local authorities the duty to set up Local Safeguarding Children Boards, which provide a means of ensuring the co-operation and effectiveness of safeguarding strategies [sec. 13].

Children and Young Persons Act 2008

The Children and Young Persons Act 2008 extends the statutory framework for looked after children in England and Wales, including placing into law some of the material found in the Care Matters white paper. Its key provisions are:

- local authorities must ensure that appropriate accommodation is provided for all looked after children and young people in its care [sec. 8];
- there must be an independent reviewing officer, who serves to ensure that the local authority is carrying out its statutory duties in regard to looked after children and young people [sec. 10];
- there must be a designated member of staff at all maintained schools, charged with promoting the educational achievement of all looked after children in that school [sec. 20];
- local authorities have a duty to provide further assistance to those children in care and care leavers under the age of 25 to pursue education or training [sec. 22].

4.2 The looked after child population

There are around 60,000 looked after children in the UK at any one time, amounting to 5% of all children and young people. Despite fewer individuals entering care in recent years, this population remains stable as many stay in care for longer – although only 13% of children and young people remain in the care system for more than five years.[8] Children and young people tend to enter and leave care as their circumstances change, and receive different forms of care depending on their needs.

Key information – looked after children (2009)

- Gender – 57% are female and 43% male.
- Age – the majority (41%) are 10-15 years old; 33% are 1-9 years old.
- Ethnicity – 76% are white; 7% black or black British; 8% mixed; 5% Asian or Asian British; 3% other.
- Mental health status – 45% of looked after children and young people had a mental disorder in 2002; 42% had a statement of special educational needs.
- Asylum seeker - unaccompanied asylum seeking children make up around 6% of looked after children and young people.[9]

DCSF (2009). Children Looked After in England.

Why are they in care?

At the time of going into care looked after children may have variety of different needs. For England, the following are the most applicable:

- abuse or neglect (61%)
- their family situation is one of 'acute stress' or 'dysfunction' (20%);
- absent parenting (9%);
- child's disability (4%);
- parental illness or disability (4%); or
- socially unacceptable behaviour from child (2%).[10]

The legislation used to take children into care is also instructive in that it suggests the urgency of the need to place the child under the supervision of his or he local authority:

8 DfES (2006). Care Matters: Transforming the Lives of Children and Young People in Care. London: The Stationery Office.pp. 14-16.
9 DCSF (2009). Children Looked After in England (Including Adoption and Care Leavers) Year Ending 31 March 2009: Statistical First Release. Nottingham: DCSF Publications.
10 Ibid.

The majority of looked after children enter care due to abuse or neglect (61% in England). The remaining children are likely to because:

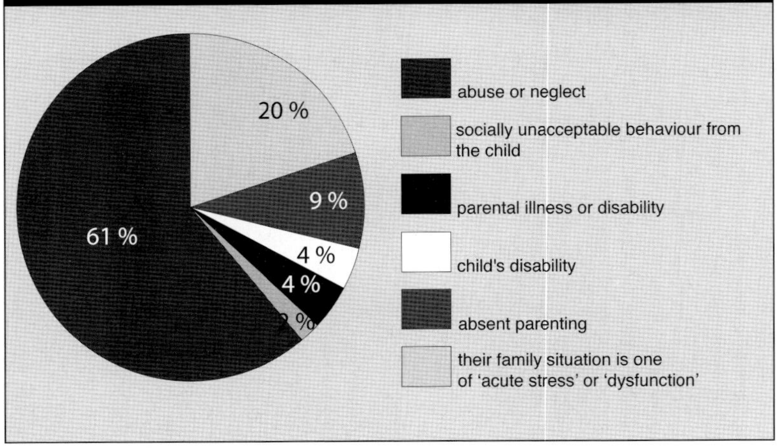

Key information – looked after children: who are they?

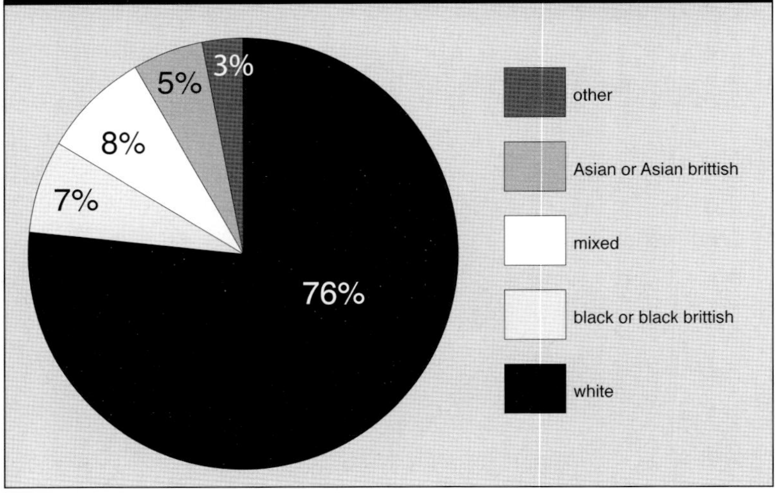

- 59% of children and young people were placed under Section 31 of the 1989 act care orders (80% of these were full care orders, where the child is placed under the care of the local authority due to concern that they are at risk of significant harm from a carer or themselves);
- 32% were placed under voluntary agreements under section 20 of the 1989 act, which means care is provided by residential or foster care in the short or long term, at the request of a family who are experiencing difficulties. The child or young person is expected to return to the family, and parental responsibility is maintained. The majority of all children who entered care did so under a voluntary agreement (66%) and were placed in a foster placement (76%);
- 8% were placed in adoption, with 62% of these adoptions being of children aged under one year;

How is their care provided?

The care experience for looked after children can vary significantly depending upon the type of setting. There are two main types of care arrangement that children may enter: fostering or residential care.

It is widely recognised that the relationship between the carer and child or young person is of considerable importance. After a period of turmoil in their personal life, looked after children are served best when their care placement is stable, and is with carers who are loving, committed and understanding.[11]

Teachers and other professionals are well situated to support the relationship between the child or young person and his or her carer. A designated teacher may, for example, take steps to maximise the role the carer plays in the child's life by maintaining regular communication and supporting them to assist the child with homework. An understanding of the distinctive challenges that different care settings are likely to present will enable a designated teacher to better meet this goal.

Fostering

In England, 73% of looked after children are in foster care, defined as a short or long term arrangement whereby children and young people are given a home.[12] Fostering describes the process whereby carers undertake responsibility for care until the child or young person can move back to their family, or on elsewhere. Under some circumstances a foster carer might go on to adopt the looked after child or young person, but this is not common.

11 DfES (2007). Care Matters: Time for Change. London: The Stationery Office, pp. 44-5.
12 Ofsted, (2009). Quality and Standards in Care, Early Education, Schools, Colleges, Adult Learning and Skills, and Children's Services: The Annual Report of Her Majesty's Chief Inspector 2008/09. London: Ofsted, p. 65.

There are different ways in which looked after children are fostered. They may be:

- in foster care if they are cared for and provided with accommodation by foster carers through the local authority;
- privately fostered if they are cared for and provided with accommodation without the involvement of the local authority by decision of the parent, child or another adult;
- in family or kinship care if they are cared for and provided with accommodation by a foster carer who is a family member or friend.

The key task of the foster carer is to create a safe and caring environment for the child to live in, and to work with other professionals around the child to ensure his or her welfare and successful development. The potential advantages of the child being in a foster placement are significant. A good foster placement will replicate the family environment giving the looked after child the kind of dedicated support and care that a normal family would. Kinship care can have the added advantage of a pre-established relationship resulting in a continuation of care, minimising disruption.

However, all foster care placements are only as good as the relationship between the carer and the child. Sometimes foster placements can break down because carers underestimate the commitment that a new addition to the household entails, or because there is friction between the looked after child and other family members, including other children. Kinship care, on the other hand, may involve elderly family members who find it difficult to cope with the different challenges that are posed by today's generation of young children.

Most adults who foster will need to meet a set of minimum standards agreed by the Department for Education and the Children's Workforce Development Council within 12 months of their being approved. These include the qualifications and skills that they will need to effectively fulfil their responsibilities to the child, and is part of a general drive to professionalise foster carers so as to put them on equal footing with other actors around the child.

Residential care

There are around 2,000 residential care homes, or children's homes as they are more commonly referred to, in England.[13] Amongst these the types of children's homes may differ substantially. They may be specialised, such as caring for children and young people who have mental or physical learning difficulties, behaviour issues, or who have suffered drug or alcohol problems.

Children's homes have received a bad press at times in the past, and the national picture is still mixed, with Ofsted reporting that only 64% are 'good' or 'outstanding'.[14] Nevertheless, looked after children have reported that there are many factors that they enjoy about children's homes, for example:

- they are able to interact with a variety of different adults, not just care staff, but cooks and cleaners;
- they can meet children and young people from diverse backgrounds, who may share the same interests and life experiences as they do;
- there are often good facilities and service provisions in children's homes which looked after children and young people may have lacked at home or in their previous placement, for example, televisions, computers and good food.[15]

However, children's homes also offer different challenges when compared to other care settings. Amongst children and young people consulted, two recurring problems include having to live with other residents that you might not get along with and being forced to abide by the rules of the children's home.[16]

13 Ofsted, (2009). Quality and Standards in Care, Early Education, Schools, Colleges, Adult Learning and Skills, and Children's Services: The Annual Report of Her Majesty's Chief Inspector 2008/09. London: Ofsted, p. 63.
14 Ibid.
15 Ofsted (2009). Life in Children's Homes: A Report of Children's Experience by the Children's Rights Director for England. London: Ofsted, p. 4.
16 Ibid., p. 5.

4.3 The care plan and care plan review

The care plan is the responsibility of the social worker and details the developmental needs of the looked after child and their plans for the future.[17] It includes details of the long term plan for the child (the 'permanence plan') which guides the support they receive, how this support will be provided, and outlines the specific desirable outcomes which can be reviewed to determine the progress made by the child or young person, their family and carers. The care plan should be seen in the context of the permanence plan's emphasis on the emotional, physical and legal stability that is needed for a durable, supportive and secure home life. This is relevant in the context of the educational achievement of looked after children given the importance of keeping the looked after child in the same school wherever possible, and ensuring that the child experiences stable, consistent and sustained support at home.

In practice, achieving permanence is likely to be a pragmatic decision based upon the needs of the child. It may involve:

- returning to the birth family when conditions support this;
- being cared for by family and friends;
- long term foster care until adulthood;
- adoption.

The role of the care plan is to detail both the day-to-day arrangements and long-term plans that are most suitable for the child, based upon information from different agencies, and the child or young person's wishes. It will also provide information on which adults can support them emotionally and during transitions, such as friends and wider family.

The child's care plan brings together information from different areas of the child's life, which are themselves provided in other plans and assessments. At different stages of the child or young person's journey through care, the care plan will include the child's placement plan, pathway plan, child protection plan, health plan, personal education plan and a contingency plan in case care arrangements fail.

The care plan review

The last stage of this cycle - the care plan review - is in practice an ongoing process and tracks the changing circumstances in the life of the looked after child's health, education and general welfare. The formal stage in this process, a meeting with relevant parties to review the care plan, is vital insofar as it monitors the progress of all aspects in the care plan in meeting the previously set objectives for the looked after child. This stage is monitored by the independent reviewing officer, who has legal responsibility for holding the local authority to account in their responsibilities for the looked after child.

The timing of the care review is set in law as follows:

- first review within 20 days;
- second review within three months of the first review; and
- third review and all reviews thereafter within six months of the previous review.

<u>The role of the designated teacher in the care plan</u>

Given the designated teacher is independently responsible for reviewing the personal education plan in between formal reviews of the care plan, it is important the school remains up to date with developments in the care plan review process. The local authority is under a legal duty to ensure the designated teacher is consulted about any changes in the child's placement that may disrupt his or her education. If in doubt, the designated teacher can check with the social worker to ensure the school has access to the fully updated care plan for the looked after child.

17 DCSF (2010). The Children Act 1989 Guidance and Regulations Volume 2: Care Planning, Placement and Case Review. Nottingham: DCSF Publications.

Charlotte's story

"Hi, my name is Charlotte. I'm 15 years old and I have been in care since 2003, but that isn't where it had started, it all began when I was very little. My dad left home when I was three months old. I have three brothers, two of which were in care like me.

"My parents weren't capable of looking after me so I was in and out of care for about four years. Two of my brothers came with me and the only thing we used for comfort was each other. We felt very alone. We had some very nasty carers and since I was the youngest I was the one who had to be most protected.

"I never really thought of being on my own and I knew that no matter what we are always going to be together, but after we went back home one of my brothers moved to live with my dad so there was only two of us left. A year later my other brother also moved in with my dad so there was only me left at home.

"In 2003 I moved back into care but I never returned home. For a while I continued to see my mum and dad but by the time I was 13 I didn't see them at all. At school this sometimes has an effect on me and I can sometimes be very silly and be rude to the teachers even though I don't intend to. I know that my problems are not the worst problems.

"I'm now in year 11 and getting ready for my GCSE exams, and college. I have these two foster carers and they are great, they look after me better and they care for my safety and freedom. I also now have two nephews and one niece who I love dearly."[18]

Who Cares? Trust

Conclusion

This chapter has set out a brief history of the care system, detailed its key components and described the place of the looked after child within it. It is important for the designated teacher to understand the legislative framework within which they, along with all other working with looked after children, are operating. Furthermore, the looked after child's previous and continuing experiences of care will differ depending upon the reasons they came into care, whether for example, through a voluntary agreement with their parents, or through a court order. The type of care placement that the child is in will also produce its own set of opportunities and challenges that the designated teacher should be mindful of, especially over everyday issues such as homework and permission slips. The care plan provides the master document through which the different parts of the care system are drawn together and made to work to support the looked after child.

What next? further reading

- DCSF (2007). Care Matters: Time for Change
- Sinclair et al. (2007). The Pursuit of Permanence: A Study of the English Child Care System.
- Ofsted (2007). Children's Messages on Care: A Report by the Children's Rights Director for England
- Care Matters Partnership online resources for designated teachers: www.carematterspartnership.co.uk

18 Who Cares? Trust. (2010). Charlotte's Story. Available online at: http://www.thewhocarestrust.org.uk/pages/charlottes-story.html.

Chapter 5

Understanding looked after children

At a glance

- The majority of looked after children are placed in care through no fault of their own and may need extra help to overcome their pre-care experiences, thrive academically and participate fully in school.
- The designated teacher needs an understanding of how abuse and neglect can affect a looked after child's behaviour so that they can be sympathetic and maintain any professional help the child receives, but should never attempt to tackle these experiences themselves.
- A national study of 5 - 17year old looked after children found that 45% have some form of mental health disorder, which can have a major impact on their attainment, social skills and well being. 37% of these are clinically significant conduct disorders whilst 12% are emotional disorders (anxiety and depression).[1]
- Many looked after children have difficulties with attachment and challenging behaviour, and can find it hard to understand how they are feeling, interact with other people and build relationships. Teachers should be aware of how to help these children participate in class effectively and achieve.
- Certain groups of looked after children will need extra support in school, such as those with disabilities, special educational needs and unaccompanied asylum seeking children.

Introduction

The majority of looked after children are in care due to factors outside of their control, predominantly abuse or neglect. These experiences can have a major impact on their ability to thrive socially and achieve in school, including enjoying good mental health and developing positive relationships.

It is important for designated teachers to develop an understanding of some of the challenges that looked after children are likely to face because of their pre-care experiences, and an appreciation of how this might manifest itself in the behaviour of the looked after child in school. In recognition of this, the statutory guidance concerning designated teachers states that:

"Everyone involved in helping looked after children achieve should:

- be aware of the emotional, psychological and social effects of loss and separation from birth families, the reasons for that separation and that some children may find it hard to build relationships of trust with adults because of their experiences;
- understand the reasons which may be behind a looked after child's behaviour, and why they may need more support than other children but the teacher should not allow this to be an excuse for lowering expectations of what a child is capable of achieving".[2]

1 Meltzer, H., Gatward, R., Corbin, T., Goodman, R. and Ford, T. (2003). The Mental Health of Young People Looked After by Local Authorities in England. Norwich: HMSO.
2 DCSF (2009). The Role and Responsibilities of the Designated Teacher for Looked After Children: Statutory Guidance for School Governing Bodies. Nottingham: DCSF Publications, p. 11.

It is important for the designated teacher to be aware of previous experiences that may potentially help or hinder development of the looked after child, and to do their best to support him or her in having the best possible opportunities to succeed in school and beyond. The job of the designated teacher is not to address the problems directly, but to ensure that day-to-day support in school is timely and effective, make arrangements and request support from professional services. The information in this chapter will lay the foundations of knowledge needed to support looked after children to achieve the best possible outcomes. The support the designated teacher can offer does not, and should not, replace the work of professionals.

5.1 Definitions

Key information

The Education Act 2002 – statutory duty on schools to safeguard and promote student welfare, including providing a safe environment at school and identifying child welfare concerns, and taking action to address them where appropriate.

Statutory guidance under the Children Acts 1989 and 2004 states that children have a right to protection from harm and aims to maximise life chances.

'Significant Harm': 'Some children are in need because they are suffering or likely to suffer significant harm. The Children Act 1989 introduced the concept of significant harm as the threshold that justifies compulsory intervention in family life in the best interests of children. The local authority has a duty to make enquiries, or cause enquiries to be made, where it has reasonable cause to suspect a child is suffering, or likely to suffer, significant harm'.[3]

Significant harm may include:

- excessively punishing a child;
- physical harm such as hitting, smacking or shaking a child;
- a child being injured unintentionally, but due to negligent care;
- emotional abuse such as constantly criticising, threatening or rejecting a child;
- sexual abuse of any form; or
- negligence through not looking after a child – not giving them enough to eat, ignoring them, not playing or talking with them or not ensuring their safety.[4]

'Abuse' is hard to quantify as it reflects society, so how abuse is perceived can change with location, cultural values, and over time, such as the attitude toward smacking and corporal punishment in schools.[5] When any practice becomes 'likely to impair the physical, intellectual, emotional, social or behavioural development'[6] of a child then it becomes abusive and a case of ill treatment.

'Neglect' is 'the persistent failure to meet a child's physical and/or psychological needs, likely to result in the serious impairment of the child's health or development'[7] and is difficult to determine. Failure to thrive is recognisable as children will not developing physically, cognitively, socially or emotionally in line with their peers, despite having no medical reason. This can be a devastating form of abuse with long term impact as it affects both physical and mental health, but the causes are often very complex and solutions difficult to define as they are linked to poverty and material deprivation.

Neglect may include failure to:

3 HM Government (2006). Working Together to Safeguard Children: A Guide to Inter-agency Working to Safeguard and Promote the Welfare of Children. London: The Stationery Office, p. 35.
4 Royal College of Psychiatrists (2004). Child Abuse and Neglect: the Emotional Effects. Factsheet for Parents and Teachers. Mental Health and Growing Up, Factsheet 19. London: Royal College of Psychiatrists.
5 Knowles, G. (2009). Ensuring Every Child Matters: A Critical Approach. London: Sage Publications, p. 78.
6 Ibid., p. 77.
7 HM Government (2006). Working Together to Safeguard Children: A Guide to Inter-agency Working to Safeguard and Promote the Welfare of Children. London: The Stationery Office, p. 38.

- provide adequate food, clothing and shelter (including exclusion from home or abandonment);
- protect a child from physical and emotional harm or danger;
- ensure adequate supervision (including the use of inadequate care-givers); or
- ensure access to appropriate medical care or treatment.

Mental health: 'Psychological wellbeing and mental health is the terminology used in the child and adolescent mental health service review and is consistent with standard nine of the Children's National Service Framework. 'Psychological wellbeing' includes emotional, behavioural, social and cognitive attributes of well-being. The term 'mental health' is in widespread use and is used as a positive concept in line with current understanding, both nationally and internationally, and is not implied to simply mean the absence of mental illness. [8]

The designated teacher should never aim to investigate suspected child abuse cases alone or attempt to intervene clinically with looked after children. There are a number of specialist practitioners who are qualified to do so and many children and young people would prefer to keep their personal and school experiences separate. The designated teacher must attempt to understand the looked after child's experiences, strengths and needs, and be able to offer them the best possible opportunities to succeed by providing them with support and services. This includes being a sympathetic, supportive and trusted adult to the child, being aware of signs of abuse and neglect and understanding the system for passing on this information properly, and being able to represent the child or young person in the school context.

What next?

- Find out from the local authority's virtual school head what mental health services are available for the pupils in your school and local area.
- Learn more about mental health services and promoting mental health wellbeing in school from a whole school to an individual level, through targeted mental health in schools, child and adolescent mental health services, national health service support and resources from the Department for Education website. [9] [10]
- Learn about the nature and specific needs of different mental health problems that looked after children on the school roll may experience, such as eating disorders and behavioural problems.
- Contact charities such as MIND and other mental health and counselling services in your area to order some leaflets so they are available to give children and carers as required.
- Use your knowledge to help other teachers understand what support is available and support looked after children in their classes
- Any concerns that a child, looked after or not, is suffering from abuse or neglect should be drawn the attention of the appropriate authorities. Designated teachers should have access to information about how to make a refer concerns into child protection services at the local authority or how to contact the the relevant department at the local police authority. Concerns may also be referred into independent bodies such as the National Society for the Prevention of Cruelty to Children.

5.2 Understanding abuse

Everyone involved in helping looked after children achieve should understand the reasons which may be behind a looked after child's behaviour, and why they may need more support than other children but the teacher should not allow this to be an excuse for lowering expectations of what a child is capable of achieving.

DCSF (2009). The Role and Responsibilities of the Designated Teacher for Looked After Children – Statutory Guidance for School Governing Bodies

In attempting to define the designated teacher's role and the parameters of his or her involvement, the importance of working in partnership cannot be emphasised enough. This will include partnerships both

8 DCSF and DoH (2009). Improving the Psychological Wellbeing and Mental Health of Children and Young People. Nottingham: DCSF Publications, p. 5.
9 DCSF (2008). Targeted Mental Health in Schools Project, Using the Evidence to Inform Your Approach: A Practical Guide for Head teachers and Commissioners. Nottingham: DCSF Publications.
10 www.educationm.gov.uk

inside and outside the school. Understanding abuse will not mean the designated teacher manages all consequences of it, but it will help them to spot the signs and ongoing effects. It will also assist the designated teacher in developing a whole school approach to meeting the needs of the child in the classroom.
Looked after children are individuals and each child, like any other, will come with their own experiences and ways of dealing with emotions and feelings. Not all looked after children suffer abuse pre-care but many of them do in one form or another. This chapter is not intended to pigeonhole looked after children but to help designated teachers to understand how pre-care experiences can impact education and learning.

Physical abuse

Physical abuse is when children or young people are physically harmed through violent actions such as hitting, shaking, burning, slapping or suffocation. This can include fabricated illnesses whereby an adult fakes or induces illness in children to make them literally or seemingly unwell to gain attention for themselves.

Indicators of physical abuse

- Injuries of any form to any part of the body;
- injuries which are not typical of other children or young people doing similar activities, such as through play or sports;
- frequent and/or unexplained injuries;
- inconsistent or vague explanations of how the injuries were sustained.

Behavioural indicators of physical abuse

- Being withdrawn, secretive, quiet and/or unable to concentrate – sometimes referred to as 'frozen watchfulness';
- being unable to do things they could previously do, such as becoming poorly coordinated;
- finding it difficult to stay awake and participate;
- unable to play and relax with their friends;
- finding it difficult to trust adults and being wary of them;
- finding it harder to deal with new situations or challenges than they used to;
- avoiding activities that may expose their abuse, such as avoiding sports or activities that discuss families and/or relationships;
- compulsive eating or loss of appetite;
- underachieving at school, or attainment changing for no apparent reason;
- being repeatedly absent;
- being uncharacteristically aggressive or abusive, having temper tantrums and being inconsiderate;
- bullying other children or being bullied;
- lying, stealing, truanting from school or getting into trouble with the police;
- siblings or knowledge of the family indicating the child may face risk at home.[11]

Sexual abuse

'Sexual abuse involves forcing or enticing a child or young person to take part in sexual activities, including prostitution, whether or not the child is aware of what is happening. The activities may involve physical contact, including penetrative (e.g. rape, buggery or oral sex) or non-penetrative acts. They may include non-contact activities, such as involving children in looking at, or in the production of, sexual online images, watching sexual activities, or encouraging children to behave in sexually inappropriate ways'

11 'Royal College of Psychiatrists (2004). Child Abuse and Neglect: the Emotional Effects. Factsheet for Parents and Teachers. Mental Health and Growing Up, Factsheet 19. London: Royal College of Psychiatrists

Sexual abuse is a serious violation, with many experiencing ongoing abuse over a length of time and being coerced into not disclosing the events through fear of what will happen to them or the perpetrator. Having experienced such traumatic treatment by adults and having held it secret for a long time, they may find it difficult to trust and need extensive and ongoing support. Sexual abuse can affect children regardless of their background and young children may not know that what is happening to them is wrong or be able to articulate what is occurring, thus vigilance about sexual abuse is important.

Behavioural indicators of sexual abuse

No one of these signs is either necessary or sufficient as an indicator of sexual abuse, but when occurring together should raise concerns.[12]

- Sudden behavioural change which is unaccounted for, change in attainment at school;
- lack of self esteem or not looking after themselves;
- demonstration of sexual ideas through their play or talk which are not age appropriate, such as behaving in a seductive or flirtatious way. This can also be expressed through drawing or written work that is sexually explicit, which is an indirect disclosure of their experiences;
- physical evidence such as remnants of blood or discharge on clothes, bruising, sexually transmitted infections or pregnancy;
- behavioural changes such as wetting or soiling themselves, experiencing tummy pains or difficulty moving or sitting down, being tired and unable to sleep
- being withdrawn, secretive, anxious, fearful or frightened – especially of physical contact;
- becoming depressed, initiating self harm, alcohol or drug use, eating disorders such as anorexia or bulimia, running away, becoming promiscuous or taking to prostitution;
- direct disclosure - it is important to recognise that children have neither the experience nor the understanding to be able to make up stories about sexual assault;
- showing an unexpected fear or distrust, or describing receiving 'special' attention from a particular adult, or referring to a new 'secret' friendship with an adult or young person.[13]

Emotional abuse

Emotional abuse "may involve conveying to children they are worthless or unloved, inadequate, or valued only insofar as they meet the needs of another person". It can also be caused by having expectations of children inappropriate for their age, either because they are "beyond the child's developmental capability, as well as overprotection and limitation of exploration and learning, or preventing the child participating in normal social interaction".[14]

With the parent or carer this may include having a poor attachment relationship with the child, or being unresponsive or neglectful towards the child's needs. They may be unreasonably critical of the child not reaching unrealistic goals, or place their own needs above those of the child. Dysfunctional family situations such as witnessing domestic violence or parental drug, alcohol or mental health difficulties may compound this. Emotional abuse can also include witnessing maltreatment of others. Although difficult to define, "some level of emotional abuse is involved in all types of maltreatment of a child, though it may occur alone".[15]

Behavioural indicators of emotional abuse

Given its pervasive nature, the majority of looked after children will have experienced some form of emotional abuse and neglect, which will have had an impact on their development and abilities. If a child has experienced another form of abuse – such as physical or sexual abuse – or witnessed abuse occurring against others, they may well have emotional difficulties such as:

12 Royal College of Psychiatrists (2004). Child Abuse and Neglect: the Emotional Effects. Factsheet for Parents and Teachers. Mental Health and Growing Up, Factsheet 19. London: Royal College of Psychiatrists.
13 Knowles, G. (2009). Ensuring Every Child Matters: A Critical Approach. London: Sage Publications, p. 77.
14 HM Government (2006). Working Together to Safeguard Children: A Guide to Inter-agency Working to Safeguard and Promote the Welfare of Children. London: The Stationery Office, p. 38.
15 Corby, B. (2005) Child Abuse: Towards A Knowledge Base. Berkshire: Open University Press, p. 97.

- faltering growth and being slow to reach developmental, cognitive or educational milestones, such as being slow learning to walk and talk or feeding problems and slow growth;
- difficulties participating positively, including being passive and unable to be spontaneous, unable to play and be creative, being easily distracted and having low attainment;
- difficulties in negotiating social relations from finding it difficult to develop close, trusting relationships where appropriate, to being over-friendly with strangers. They may find it difficult to get on with other children, and have difficulties integrating;
- behavioural indicators such as being attention seeking or oppositional, or difficult and having low self-esteem or being unhappy, anxious or fearful.[16]

5.3 Understanding neglect

As with other forms of abuse, the designated teacher is not expected to assume responsibility for managing the consequences of neglect once they have identified the signs. The designated teacher should have a good knowledge of what support is available and work in conjunction with other professionals, in and out of school, including the virtual school head. This will again help to develop a whole school approach.

Although it is not something affecting all looked after children, many have experienced some form of neglect prior to entering care. Those children will face the same challenges and present the same indicators as those suggested for other forms of abuse, especially emotional abuse.[17] For children experiencing neglect, the visible signs of maltreatment may be noticed by teaching staff and the designated teacher, and the designated senior person for child protection should take action.

Behavioural indicators of neglect

- Abnormal growth and failure to thrive, including being underweight or obese;
- recurrent infection or illness, being hungry, tired or listless;
- having an unkempt appearance including being smelly, dirty or in unsuitable or unwashed clothing;
- describing having insufficient food, heating, ventilation, sleeping arrangements or bedding in the home environment; or being at risk from dangerous or hazardous environments or animals at home;
- having attachment disorders, poor social relations including being indiscriminately friendly or aggressive;
- having poor concentration, development, attainment or low self-esteem.

Dealing with abused and neglected children

It is important to remember that the designated teacher is not a social worker, therapist or police officer; they do not have a role in providing solutions to the difficulties that a child or young person may have faced, as they require specialised support to overcome this. The designated teacher is a trusted adult, perhaps the only trusted adult, for looked after children, who may live in an environment that is very disrupted and unstable.

As such, the designated teacher needs to feel comfortable and confident to respond in the appropriate manner if a child needs to talk to them about any concerns. If a child chooses to disclose information about abuse or neglect they may be experiencing or have experienced to the designated teacher, it may be difficult for the designated teacher to respond, but they must be prepared to support the child or young person in an appropriate way, specifically in playing an active role in coordinating an effective multi-agency response.

16 Royal College of Psychiatrists (2004). Child Abuse and Neglect: the Emotional Effects. Factsheet for Parents and Teachers. Mental Health and Growing Up, Factsheet 19. London: Royal College of Psychiatrists.
17 Ibid.

5.4 Understanding attachment

The British psychologist John Bowlby introduced the idea of attachment into common usage in 1963, as part of a study on the mother-child relationship. Since then much has been written about it and its relevance to vulnerable children. The following section provides a brief guide taken from some key texts and includes practical suggestions for working with looked after children. Interested readers should consult the 'what next?' box at the end of this section, for further reading.

What is attachment?

Children need a secure emotional relationship with their main caregiver to develop physically, emotionally and intellectually. This makes them feel loved, protected and cared for in the context of a reliable and predictable relationship, which in turn forms the model of future relationships.[18] When the care a child experiences is unreliable, inconsistent, neglectful, abusive or traumatic in the first few years of life, insecure attachment of various kinds may result in lasting psychological damage.[19] This will impact on later learning and development.

Attachment difficulties are much more common amongst looked after children and are often related to experiences of growing up with abuse, neglect, poor parenting and family breakdown; all of which can cause separation from the main caregiver even if they remain living with them. The feelings of abandonment and loss are significant and can have major implications for the child's relationship building abilities. The lack of feeling loved, important and cared for can affect the child's emotional stability, thoughts, self-awareness, identity and behaviour throughout their youth and in to their adult life.

Attachment difficulties often persist even when alternative care-givers have been found and relationships have been built. Looked after children need a secure home environment where they receive love and support from responsive carers and a strong support system at school and in other community contexts to reinforce improvements in their attachment difficulties. However, this is often not possible if the child has experienced multiple and short term changes in placement, school and location and he or she has to constantly learn about new areas, renegotiate living arrangements and relationships with residential care staff, support workers and other children or young people where they live and adjust to changing friendship groups. Insecurity can lead to difficulties in creating relationships and not having somewhere to call 'home' with the people who support them – so school can sometimes be the place where ongoing support and the strongest relationships can be found.

How the child reacts to attachment is unique to every individual child and each context or challenge that occurs will elicit a different reaction that reflects how they are feeling at that point in time. As such, children may appear to 'develop' attachment difficulties when in fact these feelings are merely becoming more apparent in their behaviour. Schools can play a strong role in providing an environment that is supportive, welcoming and understanding of attachment difficulties, and this is noted in the statutory guidance for designated teachers.

How is attachment manifested?

Key information

"Most children can communicate their distress effectively by talking and explaining to those who are likely to understand and to make a difference. But for some, this kind of telling may be difficult for a range of reasons and changes in behaviour can cause others to notice that 'something is wrong'. Unresolved separations, losses and perceived abandonment are often aspects of the histories of looked after children and behaviour can reflect this."[20]

Geddes H. and Hanko G. (2006) Behaviour and the Learning of Looked After Children

18 Royal College of Psychiatrists (2004). Child Abuse and Neglect: the Emotional Effects. Factsheet for Parents and Teachers. Mental Health and Growing Up, Factsheet 19. London: Royal College of Psychiatrists.

19 Bowlby, J. (1951). Child Care and the Growth of Love. Harmondsworth: Penguin.

20 Geddes H. and Hanko G. (November 2006) Behaviour and the Learning of Looked After Children. National Children's Bureau.

Attachment commonly elicits six primary feelings or difficulties: loss, rejection or abandonment, helplessness, control difficulties, rage, and identity confusion.[21] Different children and young people can embody these physiologically, physically, emotionally and socially in different ways, and how this is exhibited in the child or young person's behaviour can change over time and circumstance.

Physiological effects

These include:

- Sudden panic or fear resulting from triggers such as sight, sound, touch or smell invoke memories; which the child or young person cannot control;
- hyper vigilance - being constantly alert for ever-present danger resulting in reduced concentration;
- difficulties sleeping or eating normally; attempts to self-harm or self- medicate through drugs or alcohol;
- avoid stressful situations by avoiding everyday activities, school itself or social interactions.[22]

Physical effects

These include:

- headaches or migraines, clumsiness, muscle tension and aching joints, or psychosomatic illnesses such as panic attacks;
- digestive and respiratory disorders due to this long-term stress, or altered spatial awareness due to being distracted, such as seeming clumsy.[23]

Emotional effects

These include:

- feeling 'different' and isolated from other children who find it easy to interact socially. This could result from not having the language to understand or describe how they feel, so they are less able to communicate effectively;
- a lack of empathy with other people's feelings as they cannot understand their own, or, conversely, they may be very sensitive to others who experience stress and become upset by this;
- reduced emotional literacy so they only know a narrow range of emotions that may be very strong, such as being extremely angry or despairing, causing them to be unpredictable and frightening to other children, and reduced ability to maintain reciprocal relationships;
- inability to experience curiosity, fun and excitement; this makes it difficult to learn and engage in education as they see no benefit to learning; difficulty in accepting praise or love due to inexperience;
- trying to be perfect and attempting to please everyone, possibly shown through never asking for help or not being able to handle criticism, or always wanting praise for all the work they do.[24]

Social effects

These include:

- looked after children and young people may have learnt to make quick decisions at the risk of losing out, and may always choose a known 'safe option' without considering other opportunities. This may be embodied through always jumping up when the bell rings, or always doing activities in a certain way or with certain partners as they feel safe;
- diminished impulse control and have unpredictable and anti-social behaviour that can be led by peers, or may conversely make it difficult to make and keep friends;
- limited their ability to build friendships, as a result of all the above;
- volatility, and unpredictability in social situation.[25]

21 Royal College of Psychiatrists (2004). Child Abuse and Neglect: the Emotional Effects. Factsheet for Parents and Teachers. Mental Health and Growing Up, Factsheet 19. London: Royal College of Psychiatrists.

22 NCB (2006). Understanding Why: Understanding Attachment and How this Can Affect Education with Special Reference to Adopted Children and Young People and Those Looked After by Local Authorities. London: National Children's Bureau.

23 Ibid.

24 Ibid.

25 Ibid.

Helping children and young people with attachment difficulties

> ***"Inclusion is a continuous process, not a state discretely achieved."*[26]**
>
> Brusling C. and Pepin B. (2003) Inclusion in Schools: Who is in Need of What?

Helping children and young people with their attachment difficulties is a challenge for the entire team supporting the child. The designated teacher is not expected to, and should not attempt to, take on responsibility for these challenges alone. They are deep rooted and require specialist support. However, the designated teacher plays a lead role in how these behaviours are interpreted and handled in school, through interactions with looked after children and advice for other teachers. Above all, it is important to remember that looked after children need support, time and consistency – and these three values can determine the success of any interventions. The table below provides a starting point for coping with looked after children with attachment difficulties.

<table>
<tr><th colspan="2">ATTACHMENT IN THE CLASSROOM</th></tr>
<tr><td colspan="2">Signs of good early attachment
• Confident to explore and learn new things;
• communicates well;
• open to others and can relate to people with ease;
• resilient to adversity but can also ask for help when it's needed.</td></tr>
<tr><td>Symptoms of poor early attachment</td><td>How these might show up in the classroom</td></tr>
<tr><td>• absence of a reliable adult in times of trouble;
• deep mistrust of adults;
• automatic 'fight' or 'flight' reaction when faced with a threat or uncertainty;
• acting out of fear and trauma rather than understanding it emotionally;
• insensitive and/or unaware of other people's feelings, or their own;
• confused distinction between right and wrong and true and false;
• hyper-vigilance – always ready to attack in response to ever presence threat of fear or uncertainty;
• profound lack of self-respect and willingness to sabotage good outcomes so that negative expectations are kept in tack;
• feeling of worthlessness and not mattering to anyone;
• denial of all fears to take control of the situation when faced with fear or uncertainty.</td><td>• defensiveness and bravado when faced with uncertainty and fears;
• inability to tolerate not knowing;
• lack of trust and respect for adults;
• little grip on the idea of continuous tasks;
• reactive and confrontational behaviour;
• extremely sensitive to what might feel extremely humiliating failures;
• inability to tolerate not knowing;
• insensitive and/or unaware of other people's feelings, or their own;</td></tr>
<tr><th colspan="2">Strategies for long term intervention</th></tr>
<tr><td colspan="2">Predictability = stability. Feeling stable means we can better cope with uncertainty and fear.
• Make good use of diary and calendar for days and weeks so all upcoming events are marked;
• pay particular attention to transitions whether they are between classrooms, buildings, primary to sec ondary schools;
• have reliable indicators or 'rituals' to mark the start and the end of each lesson;
• set structured and concrete activities in the classroom;
• be aware changes that may occur in the classroom and/or the child's life.</td></tr>
</table>

26 Brusling C. and Pepin B. (2003) Inclusion in Schools: Who is in Need of What? European Educational Research Journal, vol.2, no. 2.

Strategies for long term intervention

Boundaries = reliability. Reliable boundaries means we are less likely to fly into a rage in the face of uncertainty

- Set clear and consistent boundaries;
- base rules on response to behaviour rather than a response to the 'rejecting' the individual child;
- base rules on keeping everyone safe rather than 'bad' or 'good' behaviour;
- be consistent, both in your individual classroom and across the school.

Structure = safe.

- Pupils unable to cope with uncertainty can often benefit from a structured task such as a word search, Sudoku, or puzzles for the first five minutes of the lesson to gain control over initial uncertainty;
- emotionally vulnerable students might not like blank paper creative task as there is the fear that emotions could spill out on to the page;
- a mistrusting pupil may find it very difficult to ask for help and so want to complete tasks without help, set achievable tasks, increasing in difficulty only in stages, and use instruments if possible rather than depending on written or spoken instruction.

Geddes H. (2008) Attachment in the Classroom

What next? Further reading

- Geddes, H. (2008). Attachment in the Classroom.
- Batmanghelidjh C. (2006). Shattered Lives: Children Who Live with Courage and Dignity.
- NCB (2006). Understanding Why: Understanding Attachment and How this Can Affect Education with Special Reference to Adopted Children and Young People and Those Looked After by Local Authorities
- Cairns K. (2006). Attachment, Trauma and Tesilience: Therapeutic Caring for Children
- Bomber L. (2007). Inside I'm Hurting: Practical Strategies for Supporting Children with Attachment Difficulties in Schools United Kingdom: Worth Publishing by Louise Bomber

5.5 Understanding challenging behaviour

All children and young people can behave badly at times, but consistently challenging behaviour can be a major obstacle to both the individual's learning opportunities and those of the class they disrupt, denying the right of other pupils to learn. As such, all schools have a discipline policy that acts as both a deterrent to bad behaviour and offers clear, consistent strategies for behaviour management and sanctions for unacceptable behaviour. An expectancy of good behaviour and mutual respect must be grounded in the school ethos, and reinforced through consistent school practices for learning, teaching and behaviour management which are supported by parents and carers in the home environment.[27]

Key information

The Education and Inspections Act (2006)[28] states that teachers have power to discipline pupils for 'breaking a school rule, failure to follow instructions or other unacceptable behaviour' either in school or on a trip and this power applies to all teaching and staff with responsibilities to children including teaching assistants. Punishment for failure to comply with school rules can include:

- one-to-one admonishment;
- removal from a single lesson, class, peer group or specific activity;
- withdrawal of rights such as access to IT or lunch time privileges;
- confiscation of belongings;
- detention, suspension or exclusion.

Looked after children's own challenging behaviour can be the biggest challenge to their academic progress in school. The designated teacher has a duty to help looked after children to develop good behavioural management techniques, and represent their interests and personal circumstances if they

27 Steer, A. (2009). Learning Behaviour: Lessons Learned. A Review of Behaviour Standards and Practices in our Schools. London: DCSF Publishing, p. 3.
28 NASUWT and DfES (2006). School Discipline: Your Rights and Powers as a Teacher', Nottingham: DfES Publications.

face disciplinary measures such as exclusion. This can be particularly challenging when working with young people with complex problems, who may have attended a number of different schools with conflicting behaviour policies, which makes it difficult for them to understand what is expected of them.

What is challenging behaviour?

Key information - behaviour

Of all children, 4% to 14% experience behavioural problems, and 40% of those with conduct disorders at the age of seven to eight years will go on to offend as teenagers, whilst 90% of offenders had conduct disorders as children. Looked after children are much more likely to have behavioural problems.[29]

Behavioural problems may be the most obvious difficulty for looked after children in schools, and can manifest as verbal or physical aggression, defiance or anti-social behaviour.[30] A child with frequently disruptive behaviour will often be classified as having behavioural, emotional and social difficulties and may be registered as special educational needs due to their inability to contain their behavioural problems in the classroom.

A looked after child's ability to learn and develop as part of their social group is inhibited by the presence of emotional and behavioural difficulties. Their social behaviours are likely to demonstrate persistent aggression or anti-social behaviour, serious rule violation and defiance, theft, lying and deliberate damage to property and cruelty to other people or animals and bullying.[31]

> ***"Sometimes I do feel angry and I don't know why – please let me know that's OK so long as I don't hurt myself or others."***[32]
> Looked after child

These difficulties can be addressed at an individual, class and whole school level, and will require the attention of experts in many cases. The designated teacher can use many of these methods to develop the whole school's approach to behaviour, develop classroom strategies for teachers finding it hard to work with looked after children, and ensure looked after children are receiving all the support they need and are not unfairly punished for challenging behaviour.

What works well

Most looked after children with behavioural difficulties will receive some form of support from other professionals, however the designated teacher can apply some of the principles used in a school environment, such as skills learnt from coping with anger training. Such methods are based on cognitive behavioural therapy (CBT), which focus on problem solving rather than addressing previous experiences, as it connects thoughts to social situations and improves self-awareness and sensitivity.[33] This aims to produce changes in thinking so they can see how their feelings are a part of their environment – such as not simply 'feeling wound up' - and helps build techniques they can use themselves to change behaviour and moods. This is empowering as it gives them the ability to better regulate how they are feeling and feel confident and proud when they stay calm, but also gives them responsibility for their own actions. This is particularly important for young people as it helps them develop social responsibility which is a key life skill, whereby they understand that what they do effects other people and that this is unfair and under their control to change.

The most prominent forms of cognitive behavioural therapy for use in a school are social, anger coping skills

29 Joughin, C. (2006). Evidence Nugget: Cognitive behaviour therapy can be effective in managing behavioural problems and conduct disorder in pre-adolescence. What Works for Children group: Evidence Nugget.

30 DCSF (2008). Targeted Mental Health in Schools Project, Using the Evidence to Inform Your Approach: A Practical Guide for Headteachers and Commissioners. Nottingham: DCSF Publications, p. 35.

31 Ibid., p. 36.

32 NCB (2006). Understanding Why: Understanding Attachment and How this Can Affect Education with Special Reference to Adopted Children and Young People and Those Looked After by Local Authorities. London: National Children's Bureau, p. 12.

33 DCSF (2008). Targeted Mental Health in Schools Project, Using the Evidence to Inform Your Approach: A Practical Guide for Headteachers and Commissioners. Nottingham: DCSF Publications, p. 36.

training and problem solving skills training[34]. These aim to challenge negative thoughts the individual might have about difficult social interactions or events, and to understand why they respond the way they so. These techniques aim to help children understand why feelings may not be rational, and to find better solutions to dealing with these problems when they arise in the future. Children need to learn to understand the position, beliefs and desires of other people to understand how social situations can be seen differently by different people; this can be difficult for looked after children, many of whom have attachment difficulties which can make it hard to empathise with others.

Promoting good mental health

Looked after children experience higher risk of mental health problems and may find it harder to learn and thrive in the school environment, develop social skills and be independent. Children and adolescent mental health services and targeted mental health in schools provide support for children and young people with mental health needs. Children experiencing mental health problems in schools are generally described as having behavioural, emotional and social difficulties which may include:

- conduct disorders, for example defiance, physical and verbal aggression, vandalism;
- emotional disorders, for example phobias, anxiety and depression that may be manifested in physical symptoms;
- hyperkinetic disorders, for example attention deficit hyperactivity disorder;
- attachment disorders, for example children who are markedly distressed or socially impaired as a result of an extremely abnormal pattern of attachment to parents or major caregivers;
- substance misuse problems;
- eating disorders, for example pre-school eating problems, anorexia nervosa and bulimia nervosa; or
- post-traumatic stress disorder.

For looked after children these problems are often manifested in attachment difficulties, relationship problems and may be related to experiences such as abuse or neglect.

What works well - targeted mental health in schools (TaMHS)

Targeted mental health in schools is already in use in a number of schools and supports mental health services for children and young people within schools, aiming to coordinate mental health services and assist effective whole-school interventions, informed by best practice and sensitive to local contexts. This model aims to identify and improve existing mental health problems (tiers one and two), and provide a preventative mental health service that offers interventions in the school setting. Preventative action and comprehensive in school services not only improves mental health overall, but also attendance and attainment amongst pupils.

For a looked after child this means the school staff are more informed about the mental health problems they may be facing, and are better at identifying them and supporting the child through the educational experience.

For staff it means that they are more knowledgeable about mental health issues and are able to identify problems and assess those with difficulties before they worsen and disrupt the educational experience, for example through temporary or permanent exclusion. This model also promotes mental health in a whole-school context, develops skills in managing behaviour confidently and effectively in class which reduces staff stress levels, and gives the staff the appropriate knowledge to know when to refer children to CAMHS and other mental health actors including looked after children's nurses, special educational needs coordinator, guidance and career advisors, heads of year and the head teacher. The virtual school head has a duty to support the designated teacher including facilitating referrals, providing access to appropriate training and sign-posting to services that may be of use to the designated teacher and looked after child.

Whole school approach

Targeted mental health in schools is an important part of improving the social, emotional and behavioural aspects of the school experience which directly impact upon educational attainment. This

34 Joughin, C. (2006). Evidence Nugget: Cognitive behaviour therapy can be effective in managing behavioural problems and conduct disorder in pre-adolescence. What Works for Children group: Evidence Nugget.

Chapter 5

is provided on the basis that mental health needs are best supported as part of universal provision, with targeted support for specific needs within a tiered structure of need.

What works well – 'the ecological approach'

The ecological approach refers to the practice of viewing the needs of a child as part of the wider social context, by considering the environments and structures that they are part of – such as their family, peer group, school and wider community. By working across different levels (from the individual to the whole school), on different issues (from bullying to emotional literacy and academic support), and with different actors (including teaching staff and parents or carers) the school can provide a holistic (all round) mental health support system, with strong links to CAMHS and other services.

5.7 The needs of specific groups of looked after children

Certain groups of looked after children will require specialist support to do well in school as they have specific difficulties; such as a disability, special educational needs or being an unaccompanied asylum seeking child. Whilst this can pose a challenge to the looked after child's ability to attain in school, legislation and statutory guidance is in place that assures that these children are entitled equality of opportunity and receive the support they need. This may include specialist support workers who can help with a specific difficulty, such as a special educational needs co-ordinator, or guides on how to manage specific challenges for looked after children, such as how to welcome an unaccompanied asylum seeking child in their first days in a new school.

It is important to explain the duties local authorities and schools have to disabled children, children with a special educational need and unaccompanied asylum seeking children so the designated teacher and the school understands what different challenges these children are facing, what the law says about how they are cared for and supported and how this might impact on the way the school meets the child's needs.

Disability and special educational needs

Key information - disability

In 2005:

- there were 34,100 disabled children or young people in the UK;
- 4% of disabled children or young people in the UK were in care;
- 65% disabled children in need were boys (56% of non-disabled children in need);
- disabled looked after children were older that the average age of children in need (84% over five years, compared to 75% non-disabled);
- a higher proportion of Asian looked after children were disabled (23%) than other ethnic groups, and 38% of these children looked after due to disability were in children's homes;
- 3% of disabled children in need were on child protection registers, compared to 10% of other children in need.[35]

Disabled is understood to "identify those who have physical or sensory impairments, behavioural or learning difficulties or mental health needs who experience barriers in accessing services and are less likely to experience the same life opportunities as their non-disabled peers".[36] The term considers the impact that societal attitudes, unequal access and other environmental barriers can have on young people who have impairments and it is the aim of this guide to promote the development of services that actively work to deconstruct those barriers. This is known as the social model of disability, and underpins government legislation.

35 Data is from The Children in Need Census (2005).
36 DfES (2006). Future Positive: A Resource Guide for People Working With Disabled Care Leavers. London: The Stationery Office, p. 8.

Key information

Disability Discrimination Act 1995 - under part 4 (as amended by the Special Educational Needs and Disability Act 2001) schools and local authorities must not treat disabled students less favourably without justification and must make reasonable adjustments to ensure they are not disadvantaged compared to their peers.

They must plan strategically to increase access to schools and the curriculum over time and must produce an accessibility plan setting out how they will do this. Schools' accessibility plans must show how they will improve access for disabled pupils by:

- increasing access to the curriculum;
- making improvements to the physical environment of the school to increase access;
- making written information accessible to pupils in a range of different ways.

Disability Equality Duty - part 5A of the Disability Discrimination Act 1995,inserted by the Disability Discrimination Act 2005) places on all public authorities (including schools) a general duty, when carrying out their functions, to have due regard to the need to:

- promote equality of opportunity between disabled people and other people eliminate discrimination that is unlawful under the Disability Discrimination Act 1995 (as subsequently amended);
- eliminate harassment of disabled people that is related to their disability;
- promote positive attitudes towards disabled people;
- encourage participation by disabled people in public life;
  take steps to meet disabled people's needs, even if this requires more favourable treatment.[37]

For schools, the reasonable adjustments duty in part four of the Disability Discrimination Act does not include the provision of auxiliary aids and services: this provision is made through special educational needs statutory duties.

Summary of schools' statutory responsibilities under special educational needs legislation

Where a child has special educational needs a school has a statutory duty to:

- do its best to ensure the necessary provision is made for any pupil who has special educational needs;
- ensure where the head teacher or a nominated governor has been informed by an local authority that a pupil has special educational needs, those needs are made known to all who are likely to teach that pupil;
- ensure teachers are aware of the importance of identifying and providing for pupils who have special educational needs;
- ensure a pupil with special educational needs joins in the activities of the school together with other pupils, so far as is reasonably practical and compatible with the child receiving the special educational provision their learning needs call for, the efficient education of the pupils with whom they are educated and t he efficient use of resources;
- report to parents on the implementation of the school's policy for pupils with special educational needs;
- adhere to the special educational needs code of practice when carrying out its duties toward all pupils with special educational needs;
- ensure parents are notified of a decision by the school that special educational needs provision is being made for their child.

DfEE (1996) Education Act, sections 313, 317 and 317A

All schools should have a plan to improve accessibility for disabled pupils that includes considerations regarding the physical environment, access to the curriculum and provisions for information in alternative forms such as Braille or large print books. This aims to support disabled children and young people in participating fully in school life, and further 'reasonable adjustments' such as physical improvements including ground floor classrooms or adequate lifts and ramps for wheelchair users. Improving access to the curriculum may include changing teaching and learning arrangements, using

37 Further information about schools' responsibilities can be found in: DfES (2006). Implementing the Disability Discrimination Act in School and Early Years Settings. Nottingham: DfES Publications..

assistive learning technology or having classroom organisation or timetabling that is considerate to their needs, whilst enabling them to participate in the same manner as other pupils.[38]

The designated teacher must listen to a disabled looked after child's experiences and concerns, and advocate for improvements that need to be made to improve the school experience, especially if provisions for disability are limited. The designated teacher can appeal to their head teacher, virtual school head and local authority for provisions of any form, including suitable school transport and assisting carers in finding funding to meet additional costs. If a child or young person cannot go to school due to medical reasons or health problems, the local authority has responsibility for their continuing education, which may include home schooling.

Whilst there are unlikely to be many looked after children or young people in care with severe disabilities in mainstream schools, the responsibility for ensuring necessary provision doesn't lie with the designated teacher explicitly. However, as since the designated teacher holds responsibility in the school for improving educational attainment and needs to have an understanding of the nature of disability and the needs of disabled children and young people, they should be involved in ensuring that provisions are made and that the relevant authorities are held to account. By acting as an advocate and supporting these needs the designated teacher can champion the rights of disabled looked after children, and build relationships with other actors to provide further help and support.

Unaccompanied asylum seeking children

Key information – unaccompanied asylum seeking children

Aiming High: Guidance on Supporting the Education of Unaccompanied Asylum Seeking Children, A Guide To Good Practice - asylum seekers are 'people who flee their home country and seek refugee status in another, possibly because of war or human rights abuses, and then lodge an application for asylum with that Government.' They must meet the 1951 United Nations Convention Relating to the Status of Refugees, showing a well founded fear of persecution.[39]

There are 3 asylum statuses:

- full refugee status;
- Humanitarian Protection (this status replaced exceptional leave to remain in April 2003);
- Discretionary leave to remain (this status also replaced exceptional leave to remain in April 2003).

The United Nations High Commissioner for Refugees defined unaccompanied asylum seeking children as being 'under 18 years old and not cared for by that child's usual carers. In the event that there is no suitable adult to care for these children, the responsibility rests with the social services department local authority and the children are cared for under the provisions of the Children Act 1989.

Unaccompanied asylum seeking children represent some of the most at risk children in care, many entering the country without any adult supervision, able to speak little or no English, and having limited or disrupted education. Unaccompanied asylum seeking children may well have endured traumatic experiences in their home countries, including witnessing or being victim to violence and abuse, and may have lost parents or family and be without anyone to care for them at all.

The designated teacher and wider school should take steps to recognise and respond to the sensitivities of the child or young person's experiences, their ethnic and linguistic background and political and religious beliefs. This group of looked after children are very vulnerable, and require intensive and sensitive support from the designated teacher and school, alongside that from other services.

38 The Disability Discrimination Act (1995) and the Special Educational Needs and Disability Act (SENDA) (2001).
39 DfES (2004). Aiming High: Guidance on Supporting the Education of Unaccompanied Asylum Seeking Children, A Guide To Good Practice. Nottingham: DfES Publications, p. 3.

Understanding unaccompanied asylum seeking children

Unaccompanied asylum seeking children may have experienced persecution and great hardships in their country of origin that may have led to disturbed behaviour; this could have a major impact on their ability to benefit from schooling. Some children and young people may have lost everything – they may have been separated from or lost family and friends, lost their homes, material belongings and familiar surroundings, and experienced serious shortages of food and necessities. They may have experienced war in their home country, been arrested, tortured and possibly raped, or forced to join armies or militias. These experiences in the home country may be compounded by experiences during the asylum process. Difficult pre- and in care experiences such as these are major barriers for unaccompanied asylum seeking children and they will need to come to terms with what has happened and build skills to succeed in their new environment and rebuild their identity.

Traumatic experiences result in strong emotional reactions, which will change over time and can be supported or made much worse by the care and support received. Certain risk factors make it more likely that problems will arise that need to be recognised by the designated teacher and considered in their educational planning and the content of teaching, while protective factors can be built upon to improve their outcomes.

What works well - protective factors for unaccompanied asylum seeking children

- Strong home support from family or carers who will give them attention and provide good quality care that reinforces improvements made at school and with other services;
- an understanding of why they had to leave their home country, and a positive attitude towards being in the UK. This can be improved by maintaining a link to their homeland in some manner or continuing that in the UK through good memories, and access to people in the UK who are from their own community for support;
- personal integrity, such as high self- esteem and optimism about the future, which reinforces the chances of making friends, integrating and achieving socially and academically. Those who can come to understand their experiences through a belief system or religion can find support and overcome the past by comprehending it using values familiar to them;
- being able to build upon their abilities and skills helps UASC to focus on what they are good at, and having support to develop positive skills and talk about negative experiences helps them to gain control and build a trusting relationship that they can rely on.

How to support unaccompanied asylum seeking children entering school

The initial entry into school can be a challenging experience for unaccompanied asylum seeking children; however it is important they gain the same opportunities as other children, attend regularly and have the opportunity to develop personally, academically and socially. The failure to integrate in to school easily and happily presents the risk they will not attend and be unable to develop the skills they need to participate in society in the future. The designated teacher holds a responsibility to support unaccompanied asylum seeking children through the transition in to school and ensure their needs are met, including adaptations within school and communication with other actors.

Entering school is challenging and stressful, and from entry unaccompanied asylum seeking children should know who they can come to for advice and support, and be 'buddied' with a sympathetic pupil who can introduce them to school life. All pupils arriving mid-year need special induction procedures, to settle them happily and make learning effective within the first few weeks. Some children will come from different educational systems, and organisation, teaching styles, subjects taught and the level of formality may be different to what they are used to.

What works well - school policy induction for unaccompanied asylum seeking children

- Ensuring parents/carers are shown around the school and that possible differences in the teaching methods, how their children will be helped to learn English and particular requirements, such as uniforms and homework policies, are discussed;
- ensuring carers are informed about their rights to free school meals, school milk, travel and uniform grants;

- ensuring, wherever possible, there is an interpreter or bilingual classroom assistant when the child starts school to help them settle;
- providing training and information for all school staff involved with admissions about the background of the children;
- ensuring that all relevant staff are informed that they will be receiving a new pupil;
- ensuring each child is interviewed to assess their past educational experiences and future needs, and that this information is accurately recorded and forwarded to all relevant teaching and support staff;
- ensuring pupils receive any welcome materials such as a map of the local area, plan of the school, name of their class teacher, details of any 'buddy' or mentor and timetable;
- ensuring the pupil's progress is reassessed after a specified period, for example half a term, and that there are monitoring procedures in place;
- ensuring there are opportunities for pupils who are not coping to be withdrawn for small group tuition or mentoring.[40]

It is likely that the greatest barrier to attainment for unaccompanied asylum seeking children will be speaking little or no English which stops them from participating fully in all aspects of school life. As a result, rapid language acquisition is a priority, and needs to be sensitive to the child or young person's linguistic background that may include not having any previous contact with the English language or the Roman alphabet, not having received any education at all and not being literate in their own language.

This calls for early assessment and specialist English as an additional language teachers or bilingual classroom assistants can assist this, however classroom teachers are responsible for ensuring pupils participate in class and may rely on the designated teacher for resources and advice. The designated teacher has a duty to ensure that teaching staff adapt their classes to support unaccompanied asylum seeking children looked after children and young people, and ensure that provisions such as additional support are supplied and effective.

Advice on classroom activities, resources and information on how to help unaccompanied asylum seeking children achieve academically and integrate socially can be found in 'Aiming High: Guidance on Supporting the Education of Unaccompanied Asylum Seeking Children'.[41]

What works well – Lewisham

In a secondary school in the London Borough of Lewisham 25% of pupils have English as an additional language and 20% came to the UK as asylum seekers or refugees.

On admission to school, pupils' performance in reading is assessed using the National Foundation for Educational Research standardised assessment test. Bilingual pupils also undertake an initial period assessment within two weeks of arriving in school. This provides background information and assesses writing levels using QCA steps or national curriculum writing levels as appropriate.

Support is systematically allocated depending on pupils' level of English language skills both in class, before and after school and at lunchtimes. An induction timetable is provided for pupils' completely new to English. In the mainstream, pupils with English as an additional language's skills in speaking and listening, reading and writing are assessed using QCA national curriculum English levels.

The English as an additional language department provide a written update of progress for all pupils moving onto the main school timetable to all heads of department and heads of house. Additional targets for writing are set and monitored by the English as an additional language department and shared with subject departments. Pupils also undertake self assessment of their writing targets using a target sheet which they take to lessons and complete themselves. Considerable pastoral support is also provided both in house by activities such as peer mentoring and by the schools' regular engagement with external agencies including provision for drama therapy and counselling.[42].

40 DfES (2004). Aiming High: Guidance on Supporting the Education of Unaccompanied Asylum Seeking Children, A Guide To Good Practice. Nottingham: DfES Publications, p. 8.
41 Ibid.
42 Ibid. p, 11.

Conclusion

Every looked after child is different; their experiences will be unique as will their response to the difficulties they face. While it is important that the designated teacher has an understanding of the common issues discussed in this chapter and how these experiences may be manifested in the looked after child's behaviour, he or she should always treat each child as an individual who has the capability to succeed academically and socially with the right support.

Specific legislation assures specialist service provision for looked after children. The designated teacher should be aware of these services, ensure that they are provided and include them in the personal education plan so that every actor in the child's life is aware of what is being done to support them. Behavioural difficulties and attachment problems can take a long time to overcome and can be difficult to handle in a school context but every child deserves the chance to fulfil their potential and the designated teacher has a duty to support them in any way possible.

What next?

Find out about local sources of support to help looked after children and young people overcome their problems. There are many online resources to provide guidance on how to encourage good behaviour in the classroom and school. These include:

- The British Association of Behavioural and Cognitive Psychotherapies (BABCP) is a multi-disciplinary interest group for people involved in the practice and theory of behavioural and cognitive psychotherapy. Their website provides information on CBT courses held across the UK www .babcp.org.uk.
- The Royal College of Psychiatrists produces a leaflet for parents on conduct disorder, what the consequences may be, and how it can be managed at home, see their website at www.rcpsych.ac.uk.
- The Social, Emotional, and Behaviour Difficulties Association (SEBDA) offers information for professionals within the field on www.sebda.co.uk.
- Mind is a charity that provides mental health support, advice and campaigning, and can provide advice on any range of issues, see www.mind.org.uk.
- The Office for Disability Issues signposts relevant services and information for disability at www.officefor-disability.gov.uk.

Chapter 6

Towards a better education for looked after children

At a glance

- The personal education plan is the key tool for involving all the relevant parties in raising the educational attainment of looked after children.
- The personal education allowance provides funding for a range of services and resources aimed at raising educational attainment.
- In addition, there is a variety of extra learning support that designated teachers can make use of to improve the self-confidence of looked after children and bolster educational achievement, including one-to-one tuition and out of school hours learning opportunities.
- Extra care should be taken at times of instability in the looked after child's educational life, including transition between classes or schools, or when there is the possibility of exclusion.

Introduction

This chapter sets out the most recent data on the educational achievement of looked after children, and summarises the main reasons for the disparity between their attainment, and that of their peers, before offering some advice on improving results. The statstics are taken from the dataset on looked after children that is released annually by the Department for Education. The most recent release can be found on their website, with separate results for each local authority area. The reader should be forewarned that the statistics can make for dispiriting reading. Indeed, the barriers to promoting educational achievement can seem insurmountable in some cases, particularly because they are likely to be rooted in factors outside of the school's control. However, the subsequent sections of this chapter will offer some concrete ways in which the designated teacher can take positive steps towards helping looked after children progress in school.

Gaining a familiarity with the national picture on the attainment of looked after children is a useful exercise for three reasons. Firstly, the statistics offer a general assessment of the challenges facing looked after children, allowing schools to compare their situation to the averages for all schools. Secondly, the statistics emphasise the national nature of the challenges faced – teachers and others involved in the learning of looked after children can take comfort in the overlap between their circumstances and others, and the possibility this provides for shared responses. Thirdly, it is hoped that the information, rather than presenting grounds for despondency, can provide an impetus for change, and help to illuminate the great importance of the designated teacher's role.

Key information

"The designated teacher has a leadership role in promoting the educational achievement of every looked after child on the school's roll."

DCSF (2009). The Role and Responsibilities of the Designated Teacher for Looked After Children: Statutory Guidance for School Governing Bodies

6.1 The educational attainment of looked after children

Data published by the Department for Education has confirmed that the progress and attainment of looked after children falls substantially short of that of their peers. The main findings from recent data include:

- the educational attainment of looked after children continues to be lower than that of their peers, although there has been improvements in the last five years;
- at primary level (KS1 and KS2), less than half of looked after children reach the nationally expected standard across all subjects, although there have been improvements in recent years; and
- at secondary level (GCSE), only about one in seven looked after children achieve five GCSEs at grades A*-C (or equivalent), and recent improvements have been small.

In surveying the data, it is important to note that educational outcomes tend to matter both absolutely and relatively. Pupils' results in school demonstrate the level of skills and knowledge they have acquired, but also signal how well they are likely to do in competition with their peers for employment and higher education opportunities later in life. In supporting good outcomes, both the proportion of looked after children meeting attainment targets, and the gap between looked after children and their peers is of very real concern. On this latter indicator, the main messages from the data are that:

- the gap between looked after children and their peers is large and becomes wider as pupils progress through the key stages;
- at primary school level (KS1 and KS2), the gap between looked after children and their peers has narrowed slightly in the last five years;
- at secondary school level (GCSE), among those gaining at least five A* - C grades (or equivalent) the gap between looked after children and their peers has increased in the last five years.

Why does it matter?

Education is important for any child, but for looked after children it is of extra significance. Looked after children often face an unstable home life, even after they come into care. School or college can be a stabilising presence and provide an important setting for children to increase their sense of self-worth. Achieving good educational outcomes is an important part of this.

It is important to remember that looked after children can have low educational aspirations which are sometimes compounded by carers and teachers. Looked after children have reported that they feel adults in their life often label them as low achievers merely because of their status as looked after children.[1] If a teacher or carer has had a negative experience with a looked after child or is negatively influenced by the average attainment figures for looked after children, it is easy for stereotypes to develop which inhibit the child's progression. The effect of this can be devastating when the child comes to make decisions about plans for the future. Lack of aspiration is counted amongst the main reasons why young people fail to go on to post-16 education or training.

The Department for Children, Schools and Families has noted that attaining five or more GCSEs at grades A*-C is "increasingly seen as the basic threshold for employability".[2] As Chapter 8 explores in more detail, looked after children are more likely than other young people to not be in education, training or employment, for which lack of basic qualifications is significantly to blame.[3]

The graphs on the following two pages set out the key information on attainment for looked after children in years 2, 6 and 11 from 2005 to 2009.

1 Social Exclusion Unit (2003). A Better Education for Children in Care. London: Social Exclusion Unit, p. 30.
2 DCSF (2009). Improving the Educational Attainment of Children In Care (Looked After Children). Nottingham: DCSF Publications, p. 1.
3 Jackson, S., Ajayi S., Quigley, M. (2005). Going to University from Care. London: Institute of Education, pp. 17-18.

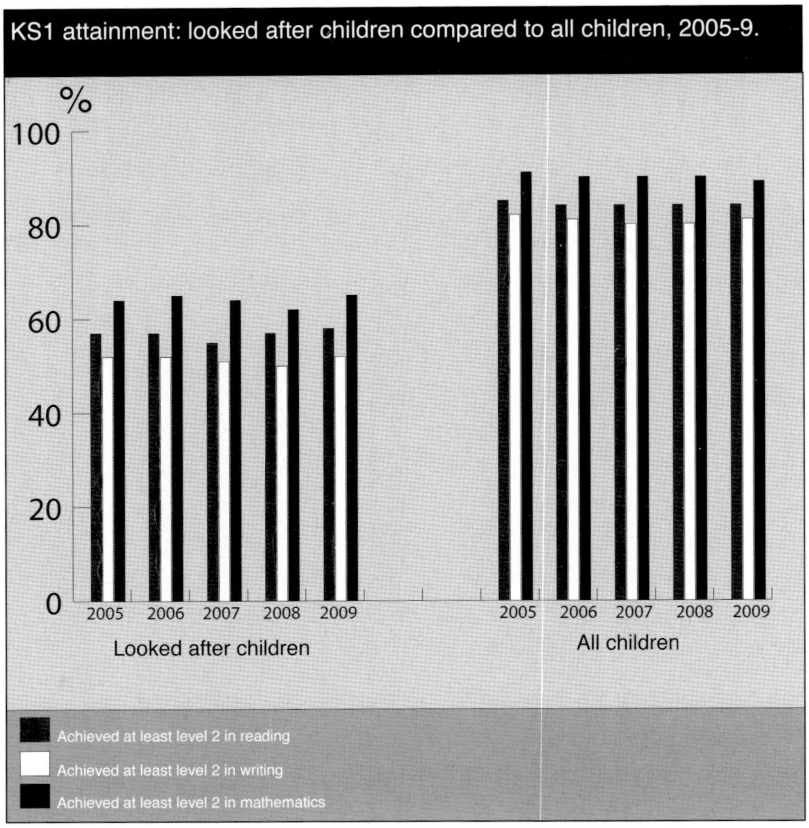

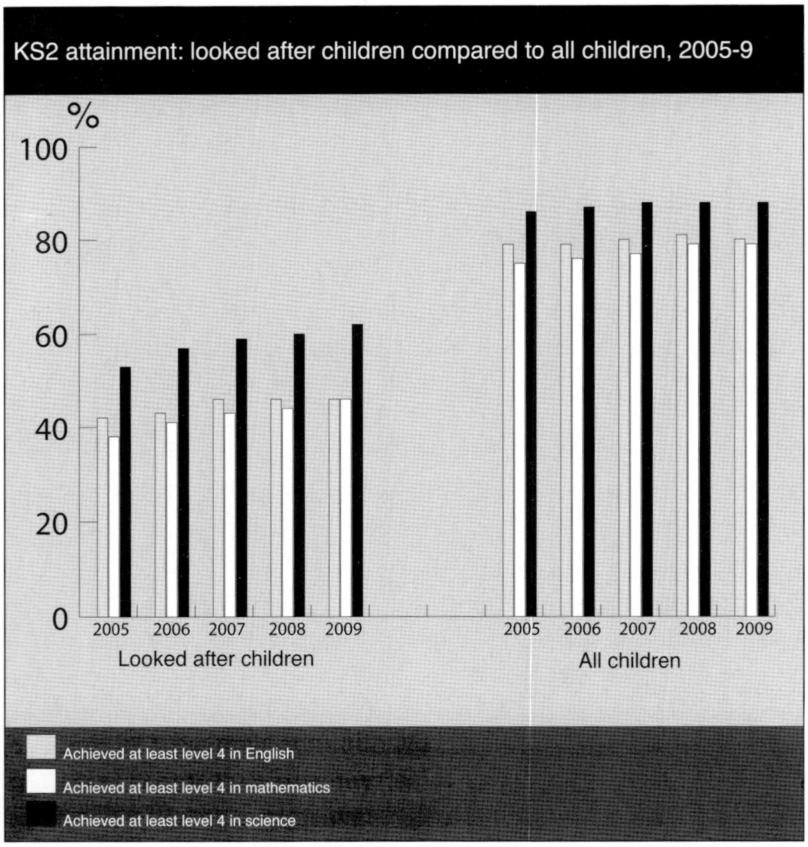

6.2 Factors explaining the difference in educational attainment between looked after children and their peers

The reasons for generally low educational achievement amongst looked after children depends as with any pupil, on the child's individual background and circumstances. However, three broad areas can be distinguished:

- the pre-care experience of the looked after pupil;
- the ongoing experiences of the looked after child outside of the school environment;
- the ongoing experiences of the looked after child in school.

The pre-care experience of the looked after pupil

"If you have family problems it may stop you doing well in your education."[4]
Looked after child

Many looked after children have experienced significant disruptions in their previous education. This may be because of time out of school for behavioural, emotional or other problems, or merely because changes in their care placement have necessitated a change in schools. The result of such instability in their educational history is likely to have impacted upon their learning; looked after children will have gaps in their knowledge corresponding to the lessons they have missed, and can then find it easy to fall behind, especially if they move to a new class or school where they are not given sufficient time to catch up. Changing schools can also impact upon factors outside of the classroom, such as lack of a stable friendship group, which can also have an effect on looked after children's attainment.

4 Ofsted (2009). Life in Children's Homes: A Report of Children's Experience by the Children's Rights Director for England

Year 11 attainment: looked after children compared to all children

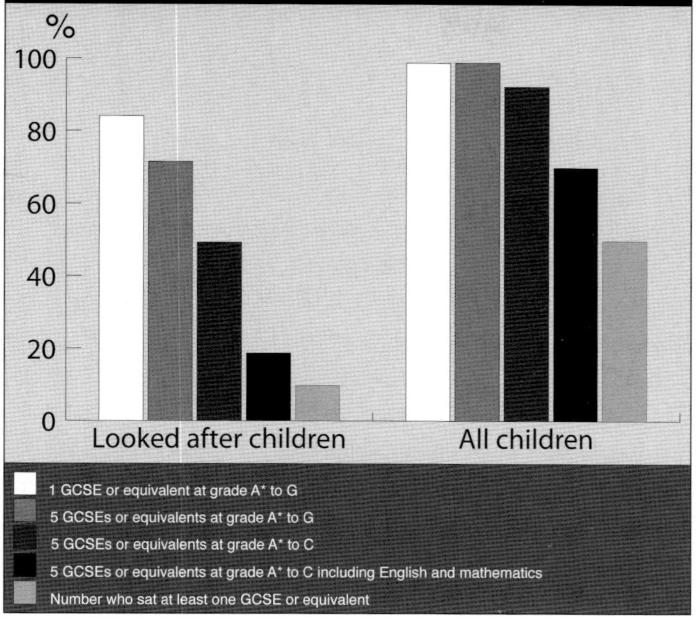

GCSE attainment: looked after children compared to all children achieving at least five GCSEs at grades A* - C, 2005-9

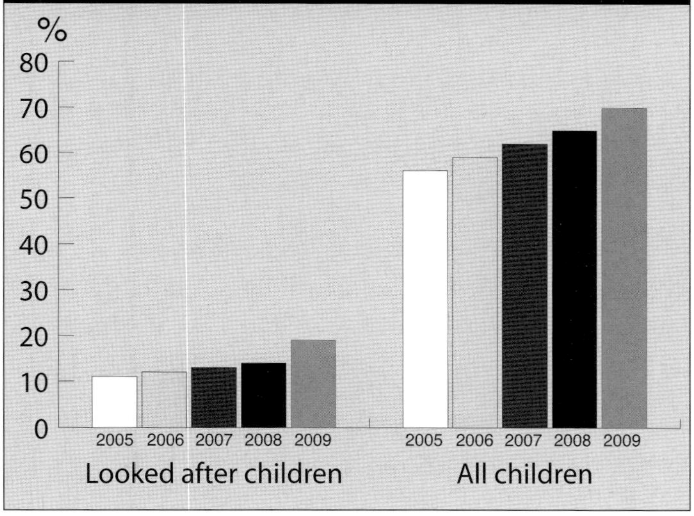

As much as 63% of looked after children have experienced abuse or neglect before they enter the care system.[5] This can take the form of lack of basic health provision, or other factors which result in poor physical or mental health, and can translate into a number of difficulties in the classroom including behaviour problems and lack of concentration.

Children may also come into care through other factors to do with the family situation, such as death, disability of a family member, or the breakdown of family relationships because of some other reason.[6] As well as potentially prompting time off school, a difficult family situation can result in long-term emotional problems for the looked after child, which may impact upon their learning. The upshot may be poor attendance, behaviour issues, or difficulties interacting with teachers or classmates.

On average, 4% of looked after children in the UK each year are placed in care due to severe disability. It is especially important that schools take seriously their duty to provide an environment where disabled children and young people are not discriminated against and where provisions are made to ensure equality of opportunity in academic, social and personal development.[7]

Key information – the education of looked after children

- At the time of the last nationwide study, half of all looked after children had a statement of special educational needs.
- 60% of all looked after children have some difficulty with reading, mathematics or spelling. Among this group, looked after children with mental health disorders were twice as likely to have significant difficulties compared to all looked after children.
- 62% of all looked after children were at least one academic year behind their age group, with a quarter of these children being three or more years behind their peers.
- Looked after children with hyperkinesis (those who find it hard to concentrate) have the highest rates of difficulty, with many having severe problems with spelling (46%), maths (45%) and reading (39%).
- Absenteeism from school was higher amongst looked after children, with 57% having been absent for at least a day during the previous term, and 18% having been absent for a week or more.

5 DCSF (2009). Improving the Attainment of Looked After Children in Secondary Schools: Guidance for Schools. Nottingham: DCSF Publications.
6 DCSF (2009). Improving the Educational Attainment of Children In Care (Looked After Children). Nottingham: DCSF Publications, p. 2.
7 DCSF (2009). Children Looked After in England (Including Adoption and Care Leavers) Year Ending 31 March 2009: Statistical First Release. Nottingham: DCSF Publications, p. 7.

- Looked after children were also more likely to truant, with teachers reporting that looked after children with a mental disorder were three times more likely to truant than looked after children without a disorder.
- Looked after children with a mental disorder were also five times more likely to get in to trouble with the police compared to other children in care, and this was dramatically higher than for all school age children.[8]

Ongoing experiences of the looked after child the outside school environment

> ***"There's very different and more rules in a care home than being with your family. I feel that I don't get the love that I need in my care home, rather than me being with my family and getting the love and affection that a young teenager would need."***[9]
> Looked after child

Looked after children often have to deal with a great deal of change and uncertainty in their lives outside of school. Care Matters: Time for Change reports that one in ten children have had more than nine placements by the time they leave care and of those children who have been in care for more than two and a half years, only 65% had been in the same placement for two years or more.[10]

This, coupled with other past and present problems, means looked after children often exhibit low self-esteem, which can translate into a lack of motivation for their school work.[11]

Carers are often not properly equipped to provide looked after children with the educational support they need outside school. This may compromise the child's ability to complete their homework, and may mean they do not receive the necessary encouragement to approach learning positively. Carers, as with parents, may also have their own education history to contend with – they may be wary of engaging with teachers, or helping looked after children with their homework because of a lack of confidence in their own academic ability.

Year 11: percentage of pupils sitting at least one GCSE compared to percentage of pupils gaining at least one GCSE

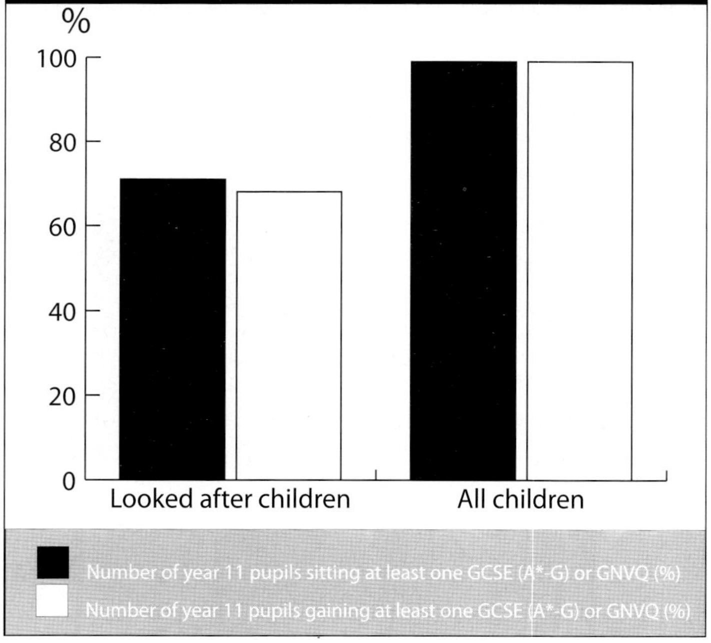

The ongoing experiences of the looked after pupil in school

Looked after children as a group are typically less likely to sit examinations than their peers. This is normally because teachers deem them not ready to be entered for examinations because of amount of lesson time missed or other impediments to their learning.

Amongst those looked after children who did sit at least one GCSE or GNVQ, the vast majority (96%) gained at least one qualification.

Looked after children tend to miss more school days than their peers. In 2008, 11.9 % of lookedd after children missed at least 25 days of school in the 12 months to September 2008, although this figure is

8 Meltzer, H., Gatward, R., Corbin, T., Goodman, R. and Ford, T. (2003). The Mental Health of Young People Looked After by Local Authorities in England. Norwich: HMSO.
9 Ofsted (2009). Life in Children's Homes: A Report of Children's Experience by the Children's Rights Director for England
10 DfES (2007). Care Matters: Time for Change. London: The Stationery Office.
11 DoH and DfEE (2000). Guidance on the Education of Children in Public Care. London: DfEE.

improving nationally.[12] A number of factors may contribute to this, including ongoing emotional or behavioural difficulties, changes in care placement or school, and truancy. Schools and local authorities often compound this problem by not being quick enough in making reparation for lesson time lost through absence.

Looked after children also often find it hard to make and sustain relationships at school due to difficulties in building or sustaining relationships in their personal life. They may therefore be more susceptible to bullying or harassment which, research has suggested, can have dramatic effects upon educational attainment.[13]

In addition, looked after children are roughly four times more likely to get permanently excluded than the national average, due to a broad combination of the other factors discussed, particularly poor relationships with teachers and classmates, and disengagement from their learning.[14] However, this figure has seen recent improvement, as the table below shows:

Exclusions: percentage of looked after children excluded compared to all children, 2005-9

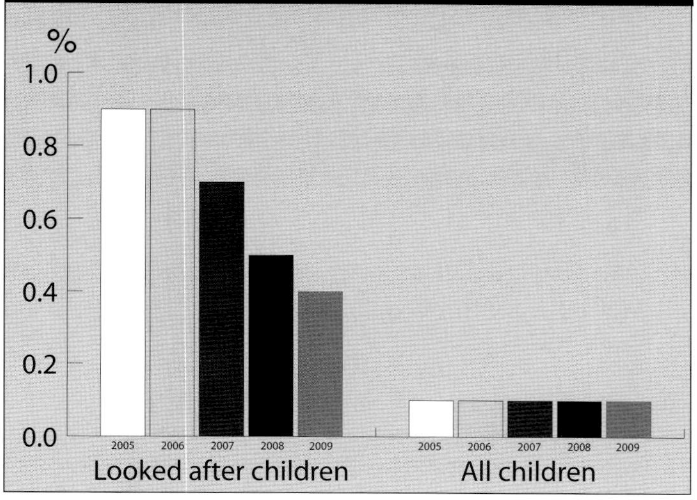

Looked after children are more likely to have special educational needs than their peers, 28% compared to 3% of all children.[15] Children are defined as having 'special educational needs' when they "have a learning difficulty or disability that requires additional support, more than is normally offered in a classroom" (DCSF, 2010, p. 6). The number of looked after children classed as requiring extra support sheds some light on the poor educational attainment figures; children with special educational needs are over three times less likely to achieve five GCSES, including English and maths, than their peers.

6.3 The personal education plan

Key information

"The designated teacher should have lead responsibility for the development and implementation of the child's personal education plan within school in partnership with others as necessary."

DCSF (2009). The Role and Responsibilities of the Designated Teacher for Looked After Children: Statutory Guidance for School Governing Bodies

What are personal education plans?

The personal education plan is the part of the looked after child's overall care plan which addresses his or her educational needs. The care plan as a whole divides the needs of the child up so the relevant professionals can ensure the right care and support is available in their area of responsibility; including health, education, emotional and behavioural development, relationships, and self-care. In dealing with the educational needs of the child, the designated teacher has a central role. The designated teacher is able to use their position in the school to rigorously monitor, develop and review the educational

12 DCSF (2009). Children Looked After in England (Including Adoption and Care Leavers) Year Ending 31 March 2009: Statistical First Release. Nottingham: DCSF Publications, p. 11.
13 Brown, S., and Taylor, K. (2005). Bullying, Education and Labour Market Outcomes: Evidence from the National Child Development Study. Sheffield: Sheffield Economic Research Paper Series.
14 DCSF (2009). Children Looked After in England (Including Adoption and Care Leavers) Year Ending 31 March 2009: Statistical First Release. Nottingham: DCSF Publications, p. 4.
15 DCSF (2010). Breaking the Link Between Special Educational Needs and Low Attainment: Everyone's Business. Nottingham: DCSF Publications.

progress of the looked after child. The personal education plan provides the means by which these activities are recorded.

What are personal education plans for?

It is important to see the personal education plan as one part of the child's overall care plan. A good personal education plan will connect with different parts of the care plan to make sure the professionals responsible for tackling other needs of the child, such as health or emotional development, and those in the local authority are aware of their role in promoting the educational attainment of the looked after child. To this end, the personal education plan addresses three areas: what the child's educational needs are, what steps are being taken to meet them, and what resources are needed to support these measures.

Two specific problems face those charged with promoting the educational attainment of looked after children. Firstly, the number of different professionals and agencies involved with looked after children typically far exceeds those involved with other children and young people. Secondly, looked after children are more likely to move care placement or school compared to their peers, and there is consequently a correspondingly higher likelihood that persons and agencies responsible for them will also change. The personal education plan is an attempt to tackle both of these problems by providing a shared resource for all those involved with the education of the looked after child, including the local authority and the school.

What information should the personal education plan contain when the designated teacher receives it?

The personal education plan should always reach the designated teacher pre-populated with some information about the child. If the child is enrolled at the school when he or she becomes looked after, then the information may be more sparse, but should include:

- the child's basic details such as age, address, and care status;
- whether or not the child has a statement of special educational needs;
- the child's carers;
- the child's parents, including any information restrictions on access to the looked after child; and
- the contact details for the child's social worker, and the looked after children education team for the local authority.

If the child was previously in care, and enrolled at another school, then the personal education plan should also come with information regarding the child's educational progress and attainment in their previous school.

What works well - tracking the attainment of looked after children

"Pupil assessment and tracking is rigorous and curricular targets are identified for all children who begin to fall behind. A range of intervention strategies are used to secure pupil progress. The approach of assessment, tracking and intervention is universal for all pupils. In addition, half-termly reports are completed for the looked after children and sent to the local authority virtual academy."[16]

Kentish Town Primary School, Camden

What information should subsequently be included in the personal education plan?

The personal education plan should contain all the information necessary to ensure that the looked after child makes good educational progress. Typically this will include the following information.

An educational needs assessment including:

- information on how data about the looked after child's progress is to be collected;

16 DCSF (2009). Improving the Educational Attainment of Children In Care (Looked After Children). Nottingham: DCSF Publications, p. 9.

- the current level of subject knowledge of the looked after child;
- any notable gaps in the child's knowledge that need addressing;
- the resources required to meet these needs.

A record of action taken to support the education of a looked after child, and objectives for the future, including:

- a record of targeted support at crucial times (e.g. before KS2 or KS4 examinations);
- a record of any other broad educational support that is given, for example one-to-one tuition, or after school clubs;
- a record of the achievements of the looked after child;
- both long and short-term personalised objectives, agreed where appropriate by the carer and the child;
- clear attainment targets;
- the action that will be taken to raise aspiration, self-confidence and ambition.

Who has responsibility for the personal education plan?

The statutory guidance concerning designated teachers is clear about the exact roles of the various professionals involved in the formulating, reviewing, and implementing the personal education plan, including the responsibility of the designated teacher and the child's social workers to develop effective partnership arrangements.

The social worker, on behalf of the local authority, has overall responsibility for setting up and maintaining the personal education plan.[17] The social worker should contact the designated teacher to set up the initial personal education planning meeting after a child is admitted into care.

Although the designated teacher should take responsibility for developing and reviewing the personal education plan, this does not necessarily mean that the he or she must personally compile the plan's content. In practice, compiling the personal education plan will be a collaborative effort, between school staff, local authority professionals, carers and the looked after child. All parties involved should ensure that the arrangements for updating and reviewing the personal education plan are working in the best possible way for the looked after child, but the division of labour between the local authority children's education service (LACES) and the school is a matter for professional discretion.

What works well

A 2008 survey by Ofsted found it is often more effective for class teachers to set and monitor targets for looked after children before consulting with the looked after child about their progress and reviewing the targets accordingly. This has two main advantages:

- firstly, in not singling the looked after child out from his or her classmates; and
- secondly in reducing the demands on the time of the designated teacher. In these cases however, it is important that the designated teacher establishes a clear division of responsibility, and maintains excellent communication with the relevant class teachers.

Ofsted (2008). Looked After Children – Good Practice In School

The designated teacher is responsible for ensuring the contents of the plan are successfully implemented within the school. This includes making sure the relevant teachers are fully aware of the looked after child's needs, and the agreed framework for meeting these needs. It may also require the designated teacher to inform them of the appropriate means of accessing extra resources or expertise, and the procedure by which they may raise concerns or suggestions about the looked after child's educational progress.

17 DCSF (2008). Personal Education Allowances for Looked After Children: Statutory Guidance for Local Authorities. Nottingham: DCSF Publications, p. 5.

The personal education plan review

Once established, the personal education plan must be reviewed at least every six months, although some schools and local authorities have seen that this is done more frequently, for example, once every school term. In addition, reviews should be carried out at times of transition, and if any educational problems require immediate attention. The personal education plan should exist in a continual state of evaluation and re-evaluation, to ensure that it remains a 'living document' – evolving with the looked after child.

The designated teacher and social worker must agree who will chair the personal education plan review. Many local authorities have a set policy on this, and in many of those local authorities the review is chaired by the child's social worker. The review should include the looked after child's carer, the designated teacher, other relevant representatives from the school and the child's birth parents if appropriate. It is vital to ensure that the child attends if they wish to. The purpose of the review is to ensure that the personal education plan is sensitive to the child's changing circumstances, including any developments at home or school that might impact upon his or her educational progress or attainment. It should include consideration of all factors that affect the education of the child, including any relevant emotional, behavioural, or social factors.

The review should be firmly geared to establishing what has been working well, identifying areas for improvement and delivering focused long and short term objectives, delineated according to who has professional responsibility for their implementation.

What next?

- In order to make sure that everyone gets the most out of the review meeting, the designated teacher should be well prepared - what challenges are affecting the looked after child's education? What extra support or resources are needed? Do the child's class teachers have any issues they would like raised?
- Be aware of any issues the looked after child might want to talk about, and ensure there is opportunity for the child to have a voice during the meeting. This is his or her chance to put forward any concerns he or she might have, for example that they are finding a particular subject difficult, or are being bullied in school.
- Think ahead to the looked after child's life in the next school term and plan appropriately – does he or she have exams coming up? Is he or she moving class or school?

The Ofsted inspection framework

In September 2009, Ofsted made some significant revisions to the way it inspects schools. A number of changes are relevant to designated teachers:

- for the first time looked after children are named explicitly as a group to whom inspectors should pay attention;
- as well as monitoring the academic performance of looked after children, inspectors will consider how the school actively promotes equality of opportunity and tackles discrimination, including staff expectations for looked after children;
- the revised framework gives more weight to the procedures schools have to safeguard all children, including looked after children, from harm;
- inspectors will also consider how the school engages with the views of parents/carers and pupils, and the effectiveness of its relationships with other providers and services;
- there is a revised self evaluation form (SEF) for schools to complete, whereby staff can self-assess how they are performing. The designated teacher should make sure that he or she has all the necessary information for looked after children to be able to complete the relevant parts of the form.

More information can be found by visiting www.ofsted.gov.ukand searching for 'school inspection framework'.

Involving the looked after child and their parents/carers in the personal education plan

The personal education plan works best when the looked after child identifies with it and feels ownership for the objectives set. However, the actual involvement of the child will depend upon a number of factors including their age, understanding and ability. It may be necessary to have the parent, carer, residential key worker or social worker act as an advocate for the looked after child for the purposes of adapting and reviewing the plan. Nevertheless, wherever it is possible, the personal education plan's content should reflect the goals and aspirations of the looked after child. As with other aspects of the personal education plan the designated teacher should ensure consultation occurs but may take the professional decision that it is best implemented by another member of staff, such as the class teacher. Most educational challenges that children and young people face cannot be effectively met without support in the home. For looked after children the advantages of a unified effort are likely to be even more palpable, and ensuring parents, foster carer(s) or residential key workers understand their role in helping the child succeed is an important part of effective personal education planning. In most circumstances, parents, carers and residential staff will have a much better understanding of the diversity of needs looked after children have and the designated teacher can use this information in deciding what strategies will be most effective in supporting educational progress.

What next?

- Be pro-active in initiating and maintaining frequent and ongoing communication between the school and carers, residential key workers, social workers and (where appropriate) the child's parents. This can involve telephone conversations, written letters and face-to-face meetings;
- parents and carers will often value involvement in the personal education planning process. Provide them with written communication, including advice on supporting learning at home and information on how to help with homework;
- the designated teacher is in a good position to demonstrate to parents and carers that the school is willing to go the extra mile for the looked after child – schools that include parents in an ethos of improvement and mutual support tend to be more successful. Keep parents, carers and residential key workers up to date with the child's progress and, where possible, consult them on changes to the child's personal education plan.

What works well - support for education in a children's home

"Claire has lived in a children's home for two years. Staff working there think education is important and have high aspirations for all children in the home. Claire normally attends school every day. On one occasion when she was excluded, the staff set her lessons and she was expected to wear her school uniform during school hours.

She is expected to do her homework each night, with one hour per night set aside as a quiet time. Staff are available to offer one-to-one help as needed. Claire participates in a variety of activities outside school including Guides and the local swimming club."[18]

What works well – explaining SATs to foster carers

In order to empower foster carers to help their looked after children in the run up to their school examinations, particularly with English and mathematics, the London Borough of Merton delivers classes for foster carers on how literacy and numeracy are taught in schools.

Different sessions are run for different key stages, and at the end, the foster carers have the chance to ask questions about what they could do to support learning at home. The carers are given packs of maths resources including cards and other learning aids for supporting education at home.[19]

6.4 The personal education allowance

In order to best support the educational progress and attainment of looked after children in accordance with the personal education plan, the designated teacher will often find it helpful to provide extra targeted resources and services. Introduced in 2008, the personal education allowance provides up to £500 per year for such extra provision.

18 Social Exclusion Unit (2003). A Better Education for Children in Care. London: Social Exclusion Unit, p. 38.
19 DfES (2006). Who Does What: How Social Workers and Carers Can Support the Education of Children in Care. Nottingham: DfES Publications.

Personal education allowances are designed to assist specifically in the education of looked after children. However, not all looked after children will be eligible. To qualify looked after children must be deemed at risk of not meeting their expected level of educational attainment.[20] This means meeting at least one of the following criteria:

- the looked after child is at risk of not reaching nationally expected attainment levels; or
- the looked after child is at risk of not making educational progress at the nationally expected rate.

The nationally expected attainment levels are as follows:

- KS1 – level two in reading, writing and mathematics;
- KS2 – level four in English and mathematics ;
- KS3 – level five in English and mathematics;
- KS4 – five A*-C grades at GCSE, including English and maths.

The nationally expected rate of progress is:

- at least two national curriculum levels in English and mathematics between in key stage; or
- during key stage 1 to make at least one level's progress in reading, writing and mathematics, dependent on the starting point.

Beyond this, local authorities may take the need of the child into consideration when deciding whether or not to allocate funding. In particular, local authorities will pay particular attention to vulnerable groups of looked after children, including looked after children who: have recently become looked after, have experienced multiple changes of school or care placement, have been placed out of authority, are in residential children's homes.
The personal education allowance is an additional allowance for supporting the education of looked after children, and the designated teacher and other relevant professional must not use funding for resources or services which should be funded under existing allocations.

Decisions about the use of personal education allowances should be framed by consideration of the kind of opportunities a good parent would spend money on to support their child's education. . See appendix III for further practical information on personal education allowances.

Accessing the personal education allowance
Personal education allowances are only granted once they have been agreed by the local authority. Normally, this will mean the local authority's looked after children education service (LACES), or the virtual school head. Accordingly, each local authority will have different criteria for accessing the personal education allowance.

The designated teacher can enhance the success-rate of applications by ensuring that the funding request is clearly linked to the assessments and objectives contained in the personal education plan. Where it is possible, the looked after child should be included in deciding what barriers to learning exist and what provision would be helpful in furthering their education.

At the next personal education planning meeting, the success of the personal education allowance in meeting the posited objective should be calculated.

What next?

- Provide children and young people clear information about how PEAs are decided and who is deciding them.
- Provide young people contact details of the person making the decision and details of how they will decide and by when.

20 See DCSF (2008). Personal Education Allowances for Looked After Children: Statutory Guidance for Local Authorities. Nottingham: DCSF Publications.

- the Department for Children, Schools and Families recommends that the the Corporate Parenting Panel should scrutinise decisions and government recommendations.
- Begin with a complete survey of the activities, resources and initiatives that are available in the local authority area and then make a realistic list of what could be provided by personal education allowance. Do this before application and decision making process begins.
- Make the whole process as participatory as possible.
- Make sure the educational benefits of the resource etc can be clearly evidenced, and are done so in the personal education plan. The clearer the educational link the more likely the application will be successful.
- Keep the decision panel as multi-agency as possible, include early years, young people, pupil referral units.
- Train designated teachers to write personal education plans and use their expertise to identify what would be of support to the young person rather than relying on Social Workers to complete these;
- Draw up clear eligibility guidelines for foster carers to follow. One local authority did this by distributing a clear flow diagrams that distinguished between resources that should come from the foster carer allowance and others that might rightly be paid for by personal education plan.

Care Matters Partnership (2010). Virtual School Head Journal

6.5 Raising aspirations

The designated teacher should have lead responsibility for promoting, and helping other staff promote "high expectations of looked after children's involvement in learning and educational progress".[21]

Looked after children are more likely than their peers to suffer from low self-esteem, including lack of confidence in their educational ability, and low aspirations for the future. This guidebook has already looked in detail at the reasons for this.

The propensity of looked after children to have low confidence in their educational ability because of previous negative experiences in their family and school lives makes raising looked after children's educational aspirations an important task for the designated teacher.

High expectations

The most important ways the designated teacher can work to raise the looked after child's confidence is by ensuring that all staff have high expectations for the looked after child's educational attainment. The negative effect of low expectations on educational attainment is well documented in the research on looked after children, and the low expectations of the adults in the child's life are one of the reasons why looked after children fail to achieve.[22]

There are a number of ways in which the designated teacher can ensure that the school has consistently high expectations for looked after children. These include:

- fully utilising the personal education plan to set aspirational targets, and review it as frequently as is necessary to ensure all relevant parties understand the objectives and are happy with the progress being made;
- ensuring there must be strong reasons for not entering a looked after child for an examination, and the designated teacher should inform the carer, the child's social worker and the governing body of the decision, and detail the reason for non-entry in the personal education plan;
- ensuring class teachers communicate to looked after children their expectations for their achievement.

A commitment to high expectations for the looked after child must be matched by support. In some cases, the designated teacher will have to deal with a difficult trade-off, mindful of both the importance of pushing the looked after child to succeed, and the danger of further denting the child's self-belief if

21 DCSF (2009). The Role and Responsibilities of the Designated Teacher for Looked After Children: Statutory Guidance for School Governing Bodies. Nottingham: DCSF Publications, p. 11.
22 See Fletcher-Campbell, F., Archer, T., and Tomlinson, K. (2004). The Role of the School in Supporting the Education of Children in Public Care. Nottingham: DfES Publications.

they feel that they are not meeting the challenges set for them. In such circumstances the designated teacher will play a key role, giving advice to class teachers and liaising with carers and other professionals to set targets at the appropriate.

What works well

"Learning mentors are a key part of the academic and emotional support offered to the looked after children. They provide one-to-one support on a daily basis if necessary and then carefully manage the transition to less regular support. Role play is used extensively to model building relationships, for example, and the mentors use activities such as art to work together and talk to the child."[23]

Torriano Junior School, Camden, London

What next? Raising aspirations

- Support looked after children to work productively with their peers, for example by being sensitive to providing opportunities for pair and group work, and choosing pairs and groups carefully.
- Ensure learning mentors discuss academic as well as emotional and social worries with the child.
- Ensure the looked after child receives praise for their achievements, while being sensitive to giving praise in ways that he or she feels comfortable with.
- Listen to the looked after child, ensuring that he or she feels empowered in their education.
- Talk to relevant staff within the school about what they think about the looked after child's aspirations, and discuss practical ways in which it can be improved.

Beyond the school

- Provide the looked after child with opportunities for extra study support at break, lunchtimes, or after school.
- Ensure that carers are informed of the educational expectations for the child as set out in the personal education plan.
- Encourage a culture of praise and reward for all of those involved with the child, including carers and other professionals.

Chapter 6

6.6 Supporting carers to help raise educational attainment

Key information

"The designated teacher should... promote good home-school links through contact with the child's carer about how they can support his or her progress by paying particular attention to effective communication with carers."

DCSF (2009). The Role and Responsibilities of the Designated Teacher for Looked After Children: Statutory Guidance for School Governing Bodies

The designated teacher is an important first point of contact for parents and carers at the school. As with other parts of the role, the government's statutory guidance does not state that the designated teacher has to personally fulfil this duty, but rather that he or she ensures it is fulfilled effectively by the school.

Under section 23 of the Care Standards Act (2000) children's home have a duty to support the looked after child's education. This includes punctuality, attendance and for the child to be suitably equipped to attend classes. For foster carers, there are National Minimum Standards for Fostering Services (2002) which also require foster carers to aid in the educational attainment of looked after children in their care.[24] The particular duties of foster carers include attending parents' evenings, open days, discussing the child's educational progress with teachers, and providing a suitable environment at home where looked after children can comfortably complete their school work and feel that learning is valued. However, significant input will be necessary from the school to make sure carers are sufficiently informed and involved about the action that can be taken to support the education of the looked after child.

23 DCSF (2009). Improving the Educational Attainment of Children In Care (Looked After Children). Nottingham: DCSF Publications, p. 15.
24 Care Standards Act 2000, (c. 14).

There are many benefits to ensuring the looked after child's educational experience is 'joined up' between home and school. Looked after children are likely to benefit from greater levels of support much more than their peers, and a good home-school relationship can help to make sure the child consistently receives the encouragement he or she needs. It also ensures, should any problems arise, they can be more effectively dealt with. Good communication is fostered by:

- making sure the carer knows who he or she can contact in the school regarding the looked after child;
- clarifying the opportunities carers have to discuss the child or young person's educational progress, or educational needs more generally;
- ensuring the carer is involved with the personal education plan and informed of any changes; and
- setting up regular written communication.

The kind of information communicated to carers will be heavily dependent upon the personal education plan, and the specific needs and objective outlined therein. However, the following are likely to be important in most settings:

- giving carers guidance on how they can better support the looked after child's learning at home, particularly supporting homework;[25]
- ensuring that the carer is appreciative of the benefits of study support for the looked after child, especially one-to-one tuition;
- information on any activities or events due to take place in the school, e.g. sports days, and how the carer can get involved if he or she wishes.

What works well

"One looked after child was unwilling to share her homework with her carer so the head teacher invited the carer to attend the homework club with the child. Homework is now provided in an envelope for the child and separately to the carer."[26]

Ward Jackson Primary School, Hartlepool

Home-school agreements

The relationship between home and school is placed a statutory footing from September 2010, when every looked after child must have a home-school agreement that outlines the respective responsibilities of both parties. Government guidance makes explicit reference to designated teachers, and charges them with the responsibility of "making sure there is a constructive and ongoing dialogue between the school and carers for looked after children".[27]

Much of the knowledge that will inform the home-school agreement will be found in the child or young person's personal education plan. The eventual home-school agreement should build upon the assessment and objectives for learning in the personal education plan in order to clarify the carer's role in pushing for educational progress and attainment. Designated teachers should see that the carer is taken through the home-school agreement in order to make sure they understand the priorities for the child's education.

The actual relationship between home and school is likely to be highly dependent upon the type of care placement it is and the particular needs of the child. Research in the area indicates that paying close attention to the social context of any home-school initiative is vital to ensuring that it bears fruit.[28]

Permission slips and parents' evenings

The school needs to be clear about which person in the child's life gives permission for activities such as

25 Ofsted (2008) Looked After Children – Good Practice in Schools. London: Ofsted.
26 DCSF (2009). Improving the Educational Attainment of Children In Care (Looked After Children). Nottingham: DCSF Publications, p. 23.
27 DCSF (2010). The Pupil and Parent Guarantees. Nottingham: DCSF Publications, p. 63.
28 See e.g. Caddell, D. (1996). Roles, responsibilities and relationships: Engendering Parental Involvement. Paper presented at the SERA conference Dundee.

school trips. It may also be necessary to clarify who pays for extra-curricular activities. If the designated teacher is unsure on either of these counts, they should contact the child's social worker for advice. It may also be useful to record key information such as this in the personal education plan where it is accessible for all relevant staff in the school. For looked after children, not being clear on these matters can mean the child missing out on valuable opportunities to build confidence and self-esteem and may further emphasise the sense of separateness that looked after children so often feel.

6.7 Providing extra learning opportunities

Key information

"The designated teacher should...make sure that looked after children are prioritised in any selection of pupils who would benefit from one-to-one tuition and that they have access to academic focused study support."[29]

DCSF (2009). The Role and Responsibilities of the Designated Teacher for Looked After Children: Statutory Guidance for School Governing Bodies

Out of school hours learning

What works well

"The school secured outreach funding for two looked after young people to participate in the Duke of Edinburgh Award. Both students had achieved bronze and were working for the silver award."[30]

Brownhills Community Technology College, Walsall

Research has shown that offering extended services for children has a positive impact on their educational attainment.[31] If properly used extended services have potential to meet some looked after children's needs effectively by providing them with new opportunities, building self-esteem and providing them with life skills.

Extended services that designated teachers might consider for the looked after children in their school might include:

- study support at break times, lunch times, after school or in school holidays;
- homework clubs;
- after school sports clubs or other extra-curricular activities;
- mentoring or 'catch-up' sessions in particular subjects;
- peer education.

As with other activities, the looked after child's participation in these services should be noted in the personal education plan. Designated teachers should be particularly mindful of any barriers the looked after child may face in accessing out of school hours opportunities because of factors such as poor transport or contact with their birth families. Any issues should be likewise recorded in the personal education plan, and all reasonable steps taken to ensure that the looked after child does not miss out on beneficial opportunities.

One-to-one tuition

Whilst most learning support appears to have positive effects on educational attainment; evidence suggests the use of one-to-one tuition can have particularly dramatic results.[32] In English for example, the reading age of participants improved by 21 months after 40 hours of one-to-one tuition.[33]

29 DCSF (2009). The Role and Responsibilities of the Designated Teacher for Looked After Children: Statutory Guidance for School Governing Bodies. Nottingham: DCSF Publications, p. 12.
30 DCSF (2009). Improving the Educational Attainment of Children In Care (Looked After Children). Nottingham: DCSF Publications, p. 22.
31 Cummings, C., Dyson, A., Muijs, D., Papps, I., Pearson, D., Raffo, C., Tiplady, L, and Todd, L. (2007). Evaluation of the Full Service Extended Schools Initiative: Final Report. Nottingham: DfES Publications.
32 DCSF (2009). Improving the Educational Attainment of Children In Care (Looked After Children). Nottingham: DCSF Publications, p. 4.
33 Every Child a Chance Trust (2006). Every Child a Reader: the First year of the National Roll-out. London: Every Child a Chance Trust, pp. 7-10.

Pilots conducted by the Department for Children, Schools and Families in ten local authorities suggested that looked after children respond better to this kind of support than their peers From September 2010 the scheme is due to be rolled out comprehensively across the country, with a programme of one-to-one and small group tuition.

The funding attached to this particular scheme is for pupils up to and including year 7, but the benefits should be considered for looked after children of all ages. While most children and young people will need to meet certain eligibility criteria for national funding, all looked after children in the relevant academic years will qualify for the scheme automatically. This entitles them to ten hours of one-to-one tuition from a qualified tutor. Local authorities may choose to use tutors from an agency, or staff within the school, although early results indicate there has been more success with the latter option.

The need for one-to-one tuition can be identified through the personal education plan. Designated teachers often find the demand for the tuition comes from the social worker, carer, or looked after children themselves.

The designated teacher, along with the social worker should ensure the tutor has all the necessary and appropriate information in order to make the most of the one-to-one tuition. Although, there may be cost implications, designated teacher should consider setting up a pre-meeting to discuss the child's particular needs. If the one-to-one tuition proves successful, the possibility of extending it using money from the personal education allowance should be discussed with the looked after child, and the relevant professionals.

What works well – online learning

There are a number of specialist materials to help support children's education at home. For example, Accipio Learning is an online teaching and learning support service for pupils who are disadvantaged, or disengaged from mainstream education. The service provides personalised, interactive lessons for full time education or study support in core GCSE subjects, work-related learning and basic skills at Key Stages 3 and 4, which can supplement education for those who need extra tuition or cannot attend mainstream school.

Lessons are delivered in an online virtual classroom with up to 15 students at a time, taught by senior subject teachers with experience in building strong relationships and working with children and young people who are harder to engage. The designated teacher can receive real-time reports on the progress of the looked after child in individual lessons, and other people involved with the looked after child - such as social workers and special educational needs coordinators – can communicate with each other.

Jenny – "My designated teacher set up online study support to help me improve my GCSE grades in maths and English, as I had fallen behind after missing school due to moving placements and having special educational needs. I have daily afterschool virtual lessons. The class is very interactive so you need to pay attention, but I enjoy talking to my classmates as we are all in the same boat and can help each other, just like normal school.

"If I had to move schools again I could keep my virtual teacher and class mates which makes me feel more secure. My foster carer helps me with my homework and we watch additional recorded lessons together online to catch up on subjects I need extra help with, which makes me feel more confident in school."

More information is available at www.accipio-learning.com

6.8 Admissions, transitions and exclusions

Admissions

> ***"They couldn't find a school that would take me because of my problems."***[34]
> Looked after child

Government legislation requires that looked after children are given priority in the allocation of school places. However, there are exceptions for certain types of school. These include: grammar schools,

34 Ofsted (2007). Children's Messages on Care: A Report By the Children's Rights Director for England

Chapter 6

schools designated as having a religious character (although if the looked after child is of the relevant faith then the priority still applies), schools that have pre-arranged selection procedures, and schools that select by banding.[35]

What works well

"A five week programme of support is provided for small groups of vulnerable children. As well as a series of visits, the personal education plans are sent to the secondary school and the inclusion manager from the secondary visits all the children in the primary school."[36]

West View Primary School, Hartlepool

Where looked after children move from one school to another, the designated teachers in the respective schools should liaise to ensure the transition is as smooth as possible, with minimal disruptions to the child or young person's education. When supervising the move of a looked after child from infant to junior school, from primary to secondary school, or in any other change of educational placement, the designated teacher should consider the following:

- well-planned induction programmes for moving to a new school (or even a new class). Looked after children might have an opportunity to make additional visits to the new school in order to get to know key staff, and get used to the new surroundings;
- primary schools can sometimes help looked after children to construct scrapbooks for saying 'goodbye' to their previous school and to say 'hello' to their new one;
- effective secondary schools often make use of a transition leader – normally a member of staff with good primary experience - to co-ordinate the induction process and to act as a bridge between years 6 and 7;
- pupils might start to visit the secondary school from year 5 onwards, familiarising themselves with specialist teachers;
- buddy systems' can be used to give year 7 pupils peer support from those in another year in the secondary school.

Chapter 6

Exclusions

"Schools are expected to proactively support and co-operate with foster carers and the local authority as a corporate parent in doing everything possible to avoid excluding a looked after child...exclusion of looked after children should be an absolute last resort." [37]

DCSF (2009). Improving the Educational Attainment of Children In Care (Looked After Children).

> ***"The school will not permanently exclude any looked after student. If necessary they use their 'inclusion centre' for internal exclusion. We pride ourselves on keeping hold of them."***
> Designated teacher

As remarked previously, a disproportionate number of looked after children are excluded from school. In the 12 months to September 2009 looked after children were four times as likely to be excluded as their peers.

The exclusion of a looked after child from school, particularly permanent exclusion, can have a serious disruptive effect on their education as well as leading to a great strain on their care placement, and general wellbeing. As a result, responsibility for reducing the exclusion of looked after children is shared amongst social workers, schools, carers and local authorities, including virtual school heads.

35 See The School Admissions (Adjudicator Determinations Relating to Looked After and Certain Other Children) (England) Regulations 2007.
36 DCSF (2009). Improving the Educational Attainment of Children In Care (Looked After Children). Nottingham: DCSF Publications, p. 24.
37 Ibid., pp. 32-3.

The designated teacher should ensure that no looked after child should be excluded without the local authority being consulted, to ensure there is suitable alternative educational provision.

The designated teacher should work with others in the school to minimise the risk of exclusions. The schools which are most successful in reducing exclusions are those that tackle the underlying causes of bad behaviour, for example:

- ensuring rules about bad behaviour should be well publicised so all parties, including pupils, staff, and parents are aware of acceptable forms of behaviour, and the sanctions for bad behaviour;
- making sure that staff apply behaviour policies in such a way that it is not perceived to be discriminatory;
- changing the looked after child's set or class.

The designated teacher should ensure the local authority is involved in any cases of potential exclusion, and liaise with other relevant professionals to secure additional support if necessary. The looked after child's social worker should be included at the earliest possible opportunity, even where the local authority does not have parental responsibility.

Furthermore, the designated teacher should advise the school governing body and relevant staff to make sure that:

- there is an understanding of the extra problems caused by excluding looked after children, and that exclusion of a looked after child only to be used as a last resort;
- there is a behaviour support plan in place as part of the personal education plan, which will aid the designated teacher and other staff in taking pro-active steps to reduce the likelihood of expulsion;
- an early personal education plan review has been called to look at the problem, and ways forward;
- the following considerations should be taken into account with looked after children if an exclusion is being considered: whether or not there has been a recent change of home placement, whether there has been recent experience of any trauma, whether or not the looked after child has any unmet special educational needs, whether the school has provided the looked after child with appropriate access to support, e.g. mentors, counselling, and a learning support unit;
- at all times the head teacher and governing body should bear in mind the Secretary of State's guidance on exclusion – Improving Behaviour and Attendance: Guidance on Exclusion from School and Pupil Referral Units (DfES, 2004). Paragraphs 51-53 are catered specifically for looked after children.

What works well - Swavesey Village College, Cambridgeshire

"In the event of an exclusion there may be a number of people connected with the looked after children who have the right to make representations and appeal, for example the child's foster carer or birth parents.[38]

The school should make special effort to ensure the looked after children has a voice throughout the proceedings, including making sure that the hearing is in a setting the looked after children feels comfortable to communicate in.

The Education and Inspections Act 2006 requires full-time education to be provided from the sixth day of the exclusion. However, the Government recommends that schools and local authorities arrange full-time education from the first day for excluded looked after children.

In the case of a temporary exclusion, there should be a reintegration interview conducted with the head of the school. For looked after children it might be helpful if the designated teacher is present at this meeting.

In the course of such an interview, the head and designated teacher (and other appropriate professionals should: stress to the parents or carers the importance of working with the school to reduce incidence of bad

38 DCSF (2009). Improving the Educational Attainment of Children In Care (Looked After Children). Nottingham: DCSF Publications, pp. 32-3.

behaviour, discuss wider problems that might be influencing the pupil's bad behaviour, discuss how behaviour problems can be addressed, agree about any steps for the continuation of the pupil's education, consider the option of a parenting contract." [39]

Conclusion

This chapter has presented the key tools available to a designated teacher in supporting educational attainment and has given an insight into the considerations that should be made when developing and maintaining the personal education plan. It is vitally important that the educational planning for looked after children is comprehensive and considers the specific needs of the looked after child. Providing tailored, timely and effective support for looked after children can greatly improve their academic outcomes and wellbeing in school.

It is important that all actors involved with the looked after child share the same priorities for the child's education. The goals of the personal education plan should be shared effectively between teachers, specialist support workers, carers and the child themselves, so that all can strive for the best possible educational outcomes.

What next? Further reading

- OFSTED (2008). Looked After Children – Good Practice In Schools
- DCSF (2009). Improving the Attainment of Looked after Children in Primary Schools: Guidance for Schools
- DCSF (2009). Improving the Attainment of Looked After Children in Secondary Schools: Guidance for Schools

39 DCSF (2009). Improving the Educational Attainment of Children In Care (Looked After Children). Nottingham: DCSF Publications, p. 21

Chapter 7

Skills for working with looked after children

At a glance

- Relationships with looked after children can take time to establish. However, strong engagement on the part of the designated teacher is key to the looked after child's academic, social and emotional development.
- The participation of looked after children in their learning is important. Where appropriate, including the opinions of the looked after child in discussions about their learning can foster empowerment, responsibility and social inclusion.
- Understanding the particular challenges that looked after children face is important in providing targeted support in school and in supporting them through transitions.

Introduction

"It really annoys me that because I'm in care everyone thinks I'm stupid. It's just an unwanted label. I try really hard and achieve at school." [1]
Looked after child

There is no separating the social and emotional development of a child or young person from their educational progress. Previous chapters have provided a detailed explanation of both why looked after children tend to achieve poorly compared to their non-looked after peers, and what the designated teacher and his or her partners can do to change this. However, in addition to providing the appropriate educational opportunities, the designated teacher is also expected to take on a more pastoral role. This will include understanding the effect that the looked after child's experiences at home may have upon his or her behaviour and learning in school, and dealing with these challenges effectively.

Some of the skills that will be employed by the designated teacher and other school staff in working with looked after children will already be a core part of any teacher's skills set. However, other skills and competencies will not. This chapter looks at the importance of involving looked after children in decision making about their education and more broadly in the school community. It describes the benefits that participation can have for looked after children and emphasises the value added by forging strong and trusting relationships. Finally, this chapter looks at supporting looked after children through transitions and explains why keeping looked after children engaged and on track through these periods is vital to successful independence in adulthood.

7.1 Relationship building

The designated teacher should build positive relationships with the looked after children within the school, and assist others in doing the same - a task which can be challenging and time consuming.

[1] DCSF (2009). Care Matters: Ministerial Stocktake Report. Nottingham: DCSF Publications.

Looked after children may find it difficult to trust or develop positive relationships. They may find it difficult to interpret the behaviour of others, and overreact to minor events, or respond to friendly behaviour with distrust. They may test the adult's limits to see if they are trustworthy, or to see if their negative presumptions about adults are correct. It is important to consider why children may respond negatively or even in a combative way to attempts from teachers to build positive relationships and to understand the importance of resilience in building these relationships.

There are a number of techniques for building positive relationships with specific children.[2] These predominantly focus on analysing the nature of the designated teacher's relationship with the child or young person, focusing on improving relationships for the long-term, and showing interest in the child's personal life. It is important to remember the importance of the whole class in improving interactions with the looked after child; daily class routines can help set a positive tone for the classroom, and create a class community that is a more inclusive and supportive of all its members.

Shared and mutual trust and respect are the basis of building positive relationships, so that looked after children can develop and engage openly with adults and their peers. This calls for positive attitudes from both adults and the looked after child, founded on a genuine commitment to the looked after child's welfare. 'Respect' in this context means valuing the identity and individuality of the child and communicating with them on their level. This will mean avoiding stereotypes, judgements and values that could distort the relationship, and prioritising their particular needs and points of view.

The designated teacher is the point of reference for handling relationships with looked after children, and their expertise may be called on for advice regarding any relationship or communication problems with a child.

7.2 Participation and inclusion

Key information - what the law says

Section 22(4) of the Children Act 1989 states that: "Before making any decision with respect to a child whom they are looking after, or proposing to look after, a local authority shall, so far as is reasonably practicable, ascertain the wishes and feelings of.. the child".

Furthermore, and although not a document of law, participation is enshrined in Article 12 of the 1989 UN Convention on the Rights of the Child. This states that parties shall assure to the child who is capable of forming his or her own views the right to express these views freely in all matters affecting the child, the views of the child being given due weight in accordance with the age and maturity of the child.[3]

The central principle of participation is listening to children and young people's views and, where appropriate, ensuring that these views are taken forwards. If adults do not take on board what children and young people say, then the involvement can become merely tokenistic, a fact which looked after children may pick up on quickly. Planning has to go in to how participation is organised, how findings will be acted upon and boundaries have to be put in place as to what changes can be made. Feedback regarding participation is essential and should be ongoing, so that children and young people know that their opinions are being taken on board and acted upon in the long run. This breeds trust, empowerment and respect, and builds confidence in being involved in participation in the future.

For looked after children, being actively involved in their own education and the school environment can build confidence and empowerment that is key to raising self esteem and aspirations. The designated teacher can encourage participation amongst looked after children and young people both in and outside of school, and can help them to make appropriate, realistic and achievable decisions about their own lives.

2 DfES (2007). Pedagogy and Personalisation: Primary and Secondary National Strategies. Nottingham: DfES Publications, p. 17.
3 Munro, E. (2001). Empowering Looked After Children. Child and Family Social Work, vol. 6, no. 2, pp. 130.

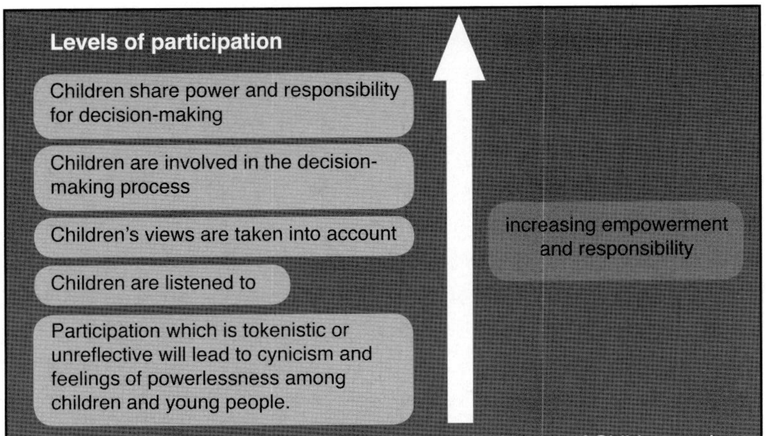

DCSF (2008). Working Together: Listening to the Voices of Children and young people.

This diagram is taken from DCSF (2008). Working Together: Listening to the Voices of Children and Young People. Nottingham: DCSF Publications.

The following principles are recommended for developing a culture of participation:

- be an active listener, take the time to sit down and really listen to what children and young people have to say;
- when talking to younger children, sit or crouch down so that you are at eye level with them;
- reflect back what children and young people communicate to demonstrate listening and check understanding;
- do not pass judgement on what they say but offer your opinions (which may differ);
- find out what they are interested in and offer something that meets these interests (e.g. bring along pictures or toys related to young children's favourite things);
- create enjoyable experiences;
- ask the children and young people what issues are of concern for them, rather than making assumptions;
- learn about group work;
- discuss activities or tasks, offer their individual strengths through discussion and observation of their individual options, and encourage them to find their preferred ways of getting involved.[4]

What works well – participation

"Working together as a team, we talked about our journeys so far since leaving care and got to know each other better, which was great for the team dynamics, as we all had different areas of strengths. We were taught about handling situations as care leavers and as trainers and did a few exercises which we all benefited from. They helped us with explaining our roles as participation assistants and our views on the care system and getting our points across clearly.

"They were also thought provoking and helped us see things from each other's point of view. We recognised each other strengths and picked things we wanted to improve on, as well as thinking about our own individual goals. We also did a session about understanding our roles as trainers, and focused on learning outcomes, which helped us recognise what we were getting out of the training."

Young person on a Participation and Voices course.

Choosing how to participate

A looked after child may need encouragement to participate in school and extracurricular activities, and the designated teacher has to support them in considering what they do or don't enjoy about their school or home environments, and what they would like to do to change this. There are often a number of different means of participation available in school; including school councils, clubs and mentoring. The designated teacher needs to be aware of opportunities and introduce different options to looked after children and young people and assist them in participating in school.

There will also be a number of opportunities outside of school, such as children in care councils, volunteering and sports clubs, all of which can offer a place where they can be involved and feel valued, and see their input having a direct affect on outcomes. These opportunities help children

4 Kirby, P., Lanyon, C., Cronin, K. and Sinclair, R. (2003). Building a Culture of Participation: Involving children and Young People in Policy: Service Planning, Delivery and Evaluation. Nottingham: DfES Publications, p. 42.

build confidence and connect to their school and community; this in turn can help maintain academic involvement and social inclusion.

Participation is also an important consideration for designated teachers when consulting on the views of looked after children in school. It is vitally important that support reflects the wishes of the user, and schools may develop looked after children and young people councils of their own, to inform more effective services and support in school. Any school council needs to have clearly defined links to the senior managing team and the power to create 'real' change, and in exchange they have a duty to represent and involve the student population in these consultations. Consultation with children and young people on a whole school level is important to build a sense of community and common purpose, and can be mobilised from an individual, group, class, year group, whole school, community or national level, such as the UK Youth Parliament[5]. Most local authorities have a pupil participation officer who can assist in creating or maintaining participation in school.

What works well – the Four Dwellings High School, Birmingham

The Four Dwellings High School, Birmingham, has linked pupil participation to school improvement through its teaching and learning discussion groups. These are made up of twelve volunteers from each year group, and meet twice a term. Twelve pupils are randomly chosen by a teacher taking into account gender, ethnicity and ability, with representation for all the tutor groups.

The work of the discussion groups, together with teachers, includes a review of the school's Improvement Plan, focussing on behaviour, feedback and assessment, professional development and extended schools. This has raised the profile and perceived importance of pupil participation in the school, particularly among teachers and governors. As a result, the school reports that pupils take greater responsibility for their learning and pupils increasingly feel that they are trusted and valued.[6]

7.3 Strategies for working with looked after children

Although many of the strategies that the teachers will use in working with all pupils in the school will be relevant when working with looked after children, it is possible to offer some general prescriptions for designated teachers to bear in mind. Many of these strategies will be directly useful in providing opportunities for educational progress as well as the more general wellbeing of the looked after child.

Key information

- The designated teacher should promote a culture in which looked after children are able to discuss their progress and be involved in setting their own targets, have their views taken seriously and are supported to take responsibility for their own learning.
- Everyone involved in helping looked after children achieve should understand how important it is to see looked after children as individuals rather than a homogeneous group and to not publicly treat them differently from their peers.

DCSF (2009). The Role and Responsibilities of the Designated Teacher for Looked After Children: Statutory Guidance for School Governing Bodies

Promoting high expectations

Holding high expectations includes not only professionals setting high standards and ambitious goals, but also expecting looked after children to hold high expectations themselves, with the suitable support and assistance. This should be part of a whole school approach to raising standards, and focus not just on academic attainment but social and behavioural skills as well. Building these skills in the early years is particularly important. Children who develop emotional literacy and self-confidence in these years are more likely to push themselves later on in their school lives.

5 See their website www.ukyouthparliament.org.uk.
6 Davies, L., Williams, C. And Yamashita, H. (2005). Inspiring Schools: Case Studies for Change – Taking up the Challenge of Pupil Participation. Esmée Fairbairn / Carnegie UK Trust.

Using individualised support for individual learning needs

A looked after child's learning needs and personal education plans need to reflect the best possible knowledge about the child's abilities and challenges - academically, socially and emotionally. This calls for consultation with the child or young person themselves, thorough assessment of their ability and information sharing with others involved in their life, such as with their social worker or previous school. This information, when shared effectively, can be used to inform personalised learning and effective holistic care. It also helps to ensure that every child is treated like an individual and that they feel valued and supported, whilst tailoring learning tasks to match their abilities and interests to improve attainment.

Treating pupil's care status with sensitivity

Where possible, target setting and monitoring looked after children's progress (academic, behavioural and attendance) should be carried out in the same way as for the wider school population; looked after children often do not want to be singled out as different or labelled as 'in care' by their peers. Rewarding instances of success may also present a difficult balancing act. It may be possible to reward looked after child publically at an awards ceremony or assembly with 'excellent progress' or 'special achievement' awards, whilst praising the particular nature of their success privately.

Setting personal and social targets

High targets for looked after children should be set and supported within the school involving other people and services as necessary. This might include targeted mental health in schools; personal, social, health and economic education and good communications with the child's carer or residential key worker. The designated teacher can take a lead role in this as the coordinator with others outside the school. As always, the progress of behavioural and social skills should be monitored using the personal education plan.

Engaging in education at a school level

The designated teacher can include looked after children in focus groups and teaching reviews, so that they can discuss their views on the school and what could be improved (although this should be done in a way that is sensitive to labelling them as looked after). This can help looked after children to build a positive, trusting relationship with other pupils, have an influence on their own education and teaching methods and establish confidence and trust in the school as 'being on their side'.

Engaging in academic, social and personal learning

Through having an active role in their personal education plan, looked after children can benefit from recognising their own strengths and weaknesses and setting personal targets for improvement. This can help fuel a sense of 'ownership' of their progress in education. The personal education plan becomes dramatically more worthwhile when the looked after child identifies with the goals set in it. The designated teacher can foster this by promoting agreement on what is expected of the looked after child.

Involving learning mentors to tackle specific problems

Learning mentors can work on specific areas to help looked after children identify weaknesses and help tackle them (usually in literacy and numeracy) or if the needs were in one specific subject, then subject teachers could provide training for this in school. By having a mentor who the looked after child can build a trusting relationship and enjoy one-to-one direct mentoring with the child can gain more in a shorter period of time and build confidence and interpersonal skills. It can be damaging for looked after children to develop a relationship with a mentor, only for the support to be withdrawn at some point (perhaps due to funding), leaving them feeling abandoned and disaffected by the learning process.

Working with looked after children

Is information about their care status treated with sensitivity?

Do they have the opprtunity to engage in school activities?

Is there extra support on offer for gifted looked after children?

Is particular attention paid to looked after children at times of instability in their school or personal lives?

Do they have access to a computer and the internet at home?

Do they have plenty of chances to give their views on school?

Promoting access to new technology

Where possible, looked after children should have access all the same learning opportunities as their peers both inside and outside school, including the internet. Access to online learning opportunities can be central to looked after children feeling included and part of their peer group. Funding for laptops and other new technology can be gained in a number of ways. The school itself may have IT resources that can be loaned, or the local authority may have a specific scheme for new technology. The personal education allowance can also be used for expenses such as laptops and appropriate software.

Supporting gifted looked after children

Many looked after children do not have the encouragement, resources or opportunities to develop special talents which would be supported by a parent in other circumstances. Pupils need to be supported and challenged by teachers who push them to make the most of their abilities, and who can provide extra resources and challenges to maintain momentum and improve their performance. The designated teacher needs to have a firm grasp of the looked after child's skills and promote their pursuit of activities and interests in the personal education plan.

Recognising communication as key to development

With schools keeping a close eye on emotional and behavioural changes, it is important that carers and family (as appropriate) are kept informed about any changes in the child's development – such as a change of teacher, or an impending school trip. Pupils also need to be aware of changes so they can prepare for them, and notifying carers can help them give assistance to the looked after child where it is needed. This should be maintained through in-depth and up-to-date note keeping about development (stored in a secure way), which can be relayed to carers via telephone, email, face-to-face conversation, or whatever form of communication is easiest for the carer.

Being responsive to needs

Designated teachers need to be responsive to immediate needs, regardless of what they are. These could range from basic needs, such as ensuring textbooks, pens and other resources are available, through to being aware of when a looked after child may need to talk through problems before lessons or gain advice and support on specific issues. The designated teacher should take seriously their role as a prominent figure in the looked after child's life, and the resulting expectations the child may have for the designated teacher to provide support and advice when it is needed.

Ensuring stability at crucial times

Years 10 and 11 are the most crucial times to ensure stability for looked after young people. Whilst studying for GCSEs, pupils are likely to resent disruption to their timetables; these upheavals can be stressful for looked after children who may already become very anxious and feel they are being further disadvantage by their being looked after. Breaks from schooling and placement moves during this time should be avoided at all costs, and children should be given an active role in any decisions.

Risk factors	*Resilience factors*
In the child • Specific learning difficulties • Communication difficulties • Specific developmental delay • Genetic influence • Difficult temperament • Physical illness • Academic failure • Low self-esteem **In the family** • Overt parental conflict • Family breakdown • Inconsistent or unclear discipline • Hostile or rejecting relationships • Failure to adapt to a child's changing needs • Physical, sexual or emotional abuse • Parental psychiatric illness • Parental criminality, alcoholism, substance misuse or personality disorder • Death and loss – including loss of friendship **In the community** • Socio-economic disadvantage • Homelessness • Disaster • Discrimination • Other significant life events	**In the child** • Secure early relationships • Being female • Higher intelligence • Easy temperament when an infant • Positive attitude, problem-solving approach • Good communication skills • Planner, belief in control • Humour • Religious faith • Capacity to reflect **In the family** • At least one good parent-child relationship • Affection • Clear, firm and consistent discipline • Support for education • Supportive long-term relationship/absence of severe discord **In the community** • Wider supportive network • Good housing and high standard of living • High morale school with positive policies for behaviour, attitudes and anti-bullying • Schools with strong academic and non-academic opportunities • Range of positive sport/leisure activities

DCSF (2008). Targeted Mental Health in Schools Project, Using the Evidence to Inform Your Approach: A Practical Guide for Headteachers and Commissioners. Nottingham: DCSF Publications, p. 29.

What works well - supporting the child or young person's development

The key principles identified in 'The Common Core Skills and Knowledge' for working with children are as follows.

Observation and judgement

- Observe and understand the motivations behind a child or young person's behaviour, so that changes can be identified, addressed and supported both within and outside school.
- This calls for active listening, record keeping, effective communication and an understanding of the subjective experience of growing up – the need to 'be able to distinguish between fact and opinion'.

Empathy and understanding

- Designated teachers must talk and listen effectively, and make sensitive judgements about what is said and what is really meant. This will involve communicating with children and young people through a medium that suits them where they are in control, such as through play.

- The ability to make autonomous decisions is important, and designated teachers can encourage them to value their own experience and knowledge and be confident in their decisions.

Knowledge

- Designated teachers need to understand the care context and relationships that the individual child experiences, and be able to advise carers on how to best support children and young people. They need to understand emotional, physical, intellectual, social, moral and character growth; how these aspects impact on each other, including attachment and how these bonds change over time.
- Designated teachers must know the boundaries of their role, who and when to pass responsibility on to relevant professionals and have a background of the laws and core policy pertaining to children. Bear in mind 'parents and carers almost always know their children best'.

Know how to reflect and improve

- Designated teachers need to be able to use both theory and experience to improve their own practices, including knowing what additional training and supervision could improve these skills. Understanding how to behave appropriately with children at different stages of development and those facing different and complex challenges is important, including knowing where to go for emotional support and advice themselves.
- Professional development includes being able to draw on experiences and insights of others, challenge previous decisions and assess actions. This includes being able to support and improve development, inspire and motivate children and young people to fulfil their potential and empower carers to support this process.

CWDC (2010). The Common Core of Skills and Knowledge: At the Heart of What You Do.

Conclusion

This chapter has set out some of the key skills and strategies that the designated teacher should make use of, both when interacting with the looked after child and when advising his or her colleagues within the school. It is important to remember that the wider development of the looked after child is likely to be at the heart of the disparity between his or her educational attainment and that of other non-looked after pupils in the class. Consequently, the pastoral role of the designated teacher becomes highly important in improving and maintaining educational progress. In this area particularly, the designated teacher will benefit from close cooperation with other partners including specialist services and the child's carers and social worker, in providing support and encouragement.

What next? - Further reading

- DfES (2007). Pedagogy and Personalisation: Primary and Secondary National Strategies
- DfES (2005). The common core skills and knowledge for the children's workforce
- DCSF (2003). Building a culture of participation: Involving children and young people in policy, service planning, delivery and evaluation'
- Care Matters Partnership online resources for designated teachers: www.carematterspartnership.co.uk

Chapter 8

Supporting the transition out of care

At a glance

- Looked after children are much more likely than their peers to not be in education, employment or training at the age of 19.
- The 'pathway plan' is the major instrument used to ensure the looked after young person's smooth transition out of care.
- Schools can assist good outcomes by spreading whole school aspirations for further and higher education.
- There are a number of government and charity schemes to assist care leavers that those involved with looked after young people should be aware of.

Introduction

> ***"Being a care leaver has to be the most pressure I've been under in my life, one minute I was 12 and living at home then I'm 21 and find myself being homeless."***[1]
> Looked after child

Care leavers are likely to experience dramatically worse post-16 outcomes than their peers. They are far less likely to progress to sixth form or university, and far more likely to come into contact with the criminal justice system, experience unemployment and live in sub-standard accommodation. [2] Of these outcomes, the number of young people leaving the care system with few or no qualifications remains of greatest concern because of the clear link this has to employability in the UK's increasingly competitive job market.

In particular, more school leavers in Britain are attending university than ever before, yet the proportion of looked after children going on to higher education remains stubbornly low.

This chapter set out the key statistics for looked after children and care leavers beyond the age of 16. It offers an overview of the leaving care process and the various actors involved in it, before setting out what schools and other professionals can do to engender better outcomes. Designated teachers should note that their role in the leaving care process itself is likely to be limited. Rather, the role of the designated teacher is to ensure that the best possible foundations are laid for the child leaving care, specifically ensuring looked after children fulfil their potential in gaining GCSEs or equivalent qualifications and promoting a culture in which looked after children are motivated to pursue further and higher education qualifications.

1 DCSF (2009). Care Matters: Ministerial Stocktake Report 2009. Nottingham: DCSF Publications.
2 See e.g. Gaskell, C. (2010). If the Social Worker had Called at Least it Would Show They Cared. Young Care Leavers' Perspectives on the Importance of Care. Children and Society, vol. 24, no. 2, pp. 136-147.

8.1 Post-16 outcomes for looked after children: the national picture

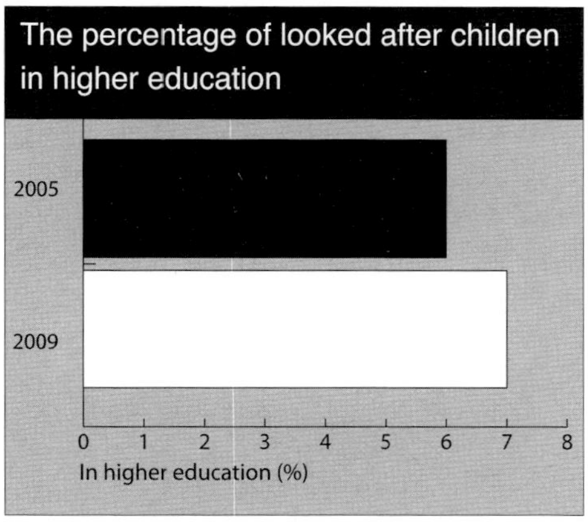

Higher education

In 2008 (2005 cohort of care leavers) only 7% of former looked after children were in higher education (i.e. post A-level study). This is up only slightly from the cohort that turned 19 in 2005, where 6% were in higher education.

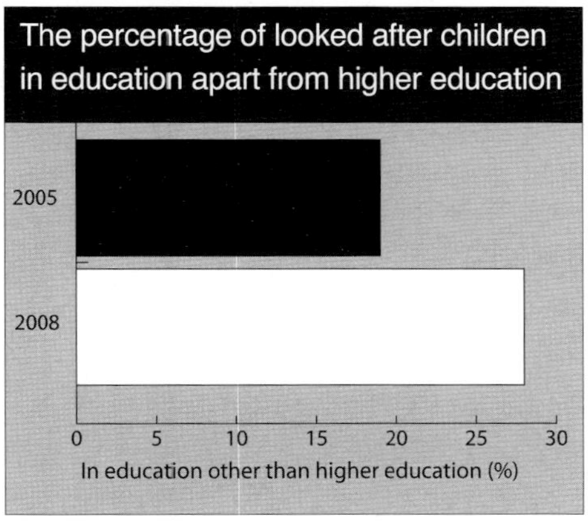

Other education apart from higher education

By 2008 (2005 cohort of care leavers), 28% of former looked after children were in education other than higher education (e.g. vocational training). This is up from the cohort that turned 19 in 2005, where 19% were in education other than higher education.

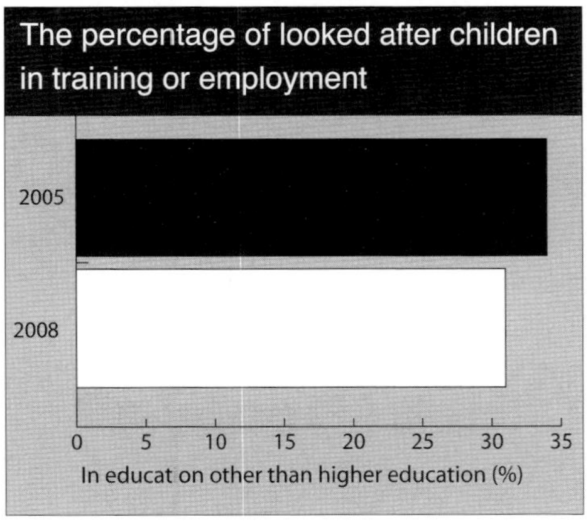

Training or employment

By 2008 (2005 cohort of care leavers) 31% of former looked after children were in training or employment. This is down from the cohort that turned 19 in 2005, where 34% were in training or employment.

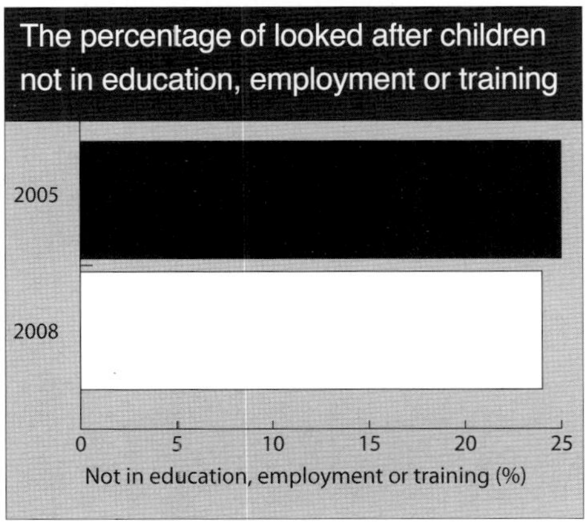

Not in education, employment or training due to reasons other than illness or disability

By 2008 (2005 cohort of care leavers) 31% of former looked after children were not in education, employment or training. This is down slightly from the cohort that turned 19 in 2005, where 25% were not in education, employment or training.[3]

3 DCSF (2009). Children Looked After in England (Including Adoption and Care Leavers) Year Ending 31 March 2009: Statistical First Release. Nottingham: DCSF Publications.

8.2 Key actors in the leaving care process

The local authority – the local authority that is responsible for the looked after child while in care will retain responsibility for him or her after they have left care, even if they move to another authority. This is to try and maintain continuity for the looked after child, and ensure that it is clear who has overall responsibility for supporting the young person at this difficult time.

The social worker – in preparation for the young person leaving care, his or her care plan will include a 'pathway plan' which will record his or her plans for education, training, or employment and the support needed to attain these goals. As with the care plan, the social worker will retain overall responsibility, and will liaise closely with the young person, his or her carer and relevant professionals to ensure effective planning.

The personal advisor – under the Leaving Care Act 2000, each eligible and relevant child is entitled to a personal advisor who will provide advice and support, and advocate on behalf of the young person to ensure the pathway plan is kept up to date and is effectively implemented.

Information advice and guidance/Connexions/careers service – These are services for young people aged 13-19, or up to 24 with learning difficulties or disabilities, to give advice and support on the transition to work and adult life. Services such as Connexions have a duty to offer information, advice and guidance to young people entering training or education to make sure they are properly qualified for employment. These services may also be available in school or from youth clubs.

Voluntary organisations – if the looked after child is being accommodated by a voluntary organisation, that organisation has an ongoing legal duty to promote his or her welfare. In addition, all professionals involved with looked after children should be aware of some of the national charities which can provide advice and support to young people, such as National Homeless Advice, and the Citizens' Advice Bureau.

The school will work to complement these actors by ensuring good working relationships with other professionals in order to makes sure all the young person's wider welfare needs are met. The designated teacher will continue to act as an advocate for the looked after child, and will play a key role in liaising with the different actors and ensuring that the personal education plan is geared towards promoting effective post-16 transitions.

8.3 The pathway plan

> ***"As I get older I can do more and take care of myself."*** [4]
> Looked after child

The pathway plan is an extension of the looked after child's existing care plan, for all looked after children aged 16 or over. It is the means by which the looked after child can plan their future aspirations and goals, and a record of the support which will be provided to ensure those goals are achieved. It will continue to be reviewed until the young person is 21, or longer if he or she remains in education.

The needs assessment

The pathway plan will be informed by a needs assessment. The needs assessment will be carried out by a range of professionals, according to their expertise in the following areas:

- health and development;
- education, employment and training;

4 Ofsted (2007). Children's Messages on Care: A Report by the Children's Rights Director for England

- the support networks available;
- financial needs;
- whether or not the looked after child possesses the necessary skills for living independently;
- care, support and accommodation needs.

As with the rest of the pathway plan, the wishes of the child or young person should be taken into account when conducting the needs assessment. This does not mean that he or she has a veto over any proposals but that it is important to consider the disadvantage the process is placed at by alienating the child or young person.

What does the pathway plan cover?
The contents of the pathway plan can be divided up into nine parts. Not all are of direct concern to the designated teacher, but he or she should consider the ways in which the school can help to meet these goals, and how his or her knowledge of the child or young person can help inform the plan.[5]

Personal support
The young person may well require support in the transition out of care and in dealing with the demands of their post-care environment. A personal advisor will play the major role in providing this personal support The pathway planning process should look to identify further assistance, for example current or past carers, family members, mentors, or friends. Specific commitment involving these people should be written into the pathway plan.

Accommodation
It is widely recognised that there is a strong link between suitable accommodation and good outcomes for care leavers. For example, the Social Exclusion Task Force found that of a group of care leavers in Norfolk, the position of 75% of those not in education, employment or training was directly linked to poor accommodation. All children classed as either 'eligible' or 'relevant' (see the glossary) are entitled to accommodation provided by the local authority.[6]

Education and training
In addition to ensuring that care leavers are in a stable placement which does not inhibit any desire they might have to pursue further education or training, the pathway plan should include steps that can be taken to promote learning for the future. This might include arranging remedial classes to boost grades, or helping the young person to access lifelong learning schemes. The designated teacher will be able to advise on what further learning opportunities will be of benefit, given his or her knowledge of the child's education thus far.

5 For more information, see the Children (Leaving Care) Act 2000: Regulations and Guidance.
6 Social Exclusion Task Force (2009). Realising Young Potential: Supporting Care Leavers Into Education, Employment and Training. London: Cabinet Office.

Employment
The pathway plan should make clear how the local authority will help the young person into employment, or help them take positive steps towards seeking employment. This will include detailing the young person's achievements – a task in which the designated teacher's input is likely to be key – and identifying future ways to improve their employability.

Skills
It may be that the young person has not cultivated the necessary practical skills to successfully make the transition out of care. In particular, the pathway plan considers three skill sets which will inform the decision as to whether or not the child is ready to leave care. These are:

- self-care skills such as personal hygiene and sexual health;
- practical skills such as personal budgeting and shopping;
- interpersonal skills such as those pertaining to relationships and sexuality.

Financial support
The financial arrangements for the young person leaving care are a crucial part of the pathway plan; all aspects of the plan should be costed to ensure they are viable, and that an accurate picture is being presented of the support that will be offered to the young person upon leaving care. Financial assistance that may be applicable to care leavers includes: higher education bursaries, scholarships and grants, and accommodation provision.

Health needs
Based upon the rigorous health appraisal in the needs assessment, the pathway plan will provide an outline of how these needs will be met. It might include information on the health benefits that young care leavers are entitled to, such as free prescriptions, or construct a timeline for how the young person will be supported to take responsibility for their own health needs.

Contingency planning
It is a truism that even the best laid plans go astray, and no matter how comprehensive the pathway plan, there should be provision for dealing with unexpected contingencies, including breakdowns in the young person's accommodation, learning or social relationships which may leave them vulnerable. Contingency planning may be made more difficult by the particular circumstances of the young person, and care may need to be taken to address his or her feelings of failure if he or she needs extra assistance after leaving care.

What next?

- Discuss with the looked after child his or her plans for the future, and encourage them to look at the different pathways available to them – including further and higher education.
- Think about the looked after child's learning goals in the context of their plans for the future and whether they need to gain particular qualifications or grades?
- Consider what extra learning support can be given to the looked after child to motivate interests for the future, or help him or her study for key examinations e.g. GCSEs.
- Ensure there is good communication between the designated teacher, the looked after child's personal advisor and social worker over effective planning for the future.

What is the role of the personal advisor?
The personal advisor is the key professional responsible for overseeing the successful development of the pathway plan, and will normally maintain contact with the young person from the age of 16 right up until they are 21. To reflect the important role that personal advisors play in ensuring smooth transitions out of care, the provision of a personal advisor to every care leaver is a legal duty of the responsible local authority.[7]

7 See further: Children (Leaving Care) Act 2000, section 6.

Personal advisors may have different titles depending upon the local authority in question; they have been variously referred to as young person's advisors, pathway advisors and careers advisors. The role has changed slightly over the decade since the Children (Leaving Care) Act 2000, with efforts to better define the job of the personal advisor and its relationship to other services. In particular, designated teachers should be aware that the personal advisor need not be a social worker although he or she should have intimate knowledge of the relevant legislation and of the necessary skills for working with young people. The division of responsibility between the personal advisor and social worker will vary depending upon particular circumstances; given that the pathway plan is an extension of the care plan it will make sense in some cases for the personal advisor to play only a restricted part, although he or she should always makes sure the plan is feasible.

Also, the personal advisor may not be part of Connexions, although even if they are not they will have close links to that service. The looked after child's pre-16 Connexions advisor may well go on to become his or her personal advisor, but this does not happen in all cases.

The personal advisor's role includes the following key elements:

- **providing advice and support** – the personal advisor will provide advice and support only as necessary for each young person. In circumstances where the young person has good relationships with his or her teachers, carers and/or mentors, the personal advisor's advice-giving role will only be limited;
- **participating in the assessment and preparation of the pathway plan** – the personal advisor's central role here will be to work with the social worker and other professionals, including those from the school, to ensure that the content of the pathway plan can be delivered once the child leaves care;
- **participating in the review of the pathway plan** – as with the care plan, the pathway plan will be subject to regular review in order to make sure that it is continuing to be effective. The pathway plan will be reviewed every six months until the young person is 21, or later if he or she is still enrolled upon an agreed education or training course. The review process will make sure that the young person is on track, and has the appropriate support (including financial support) to meet the goals set out in the pathway plan;
- **communicating with other parties to make the pathway plan a success** – the personal advisor will be the hub through which the various relevant agencies coordinate to ensure the young person is aware of and is receiving the necessary support. This will include liaising with the local authority so they are satisfied the young person is making the requisite progress;
- **keeping in touch with the care leaver** – the personal advisor should keep in regular contact with the young person and the appropriate agencies, and keep written records of this contact. Apart from this being necessary to prove that all the required legal duties are being carried out, the young person may find these records useful at a later date.

8.4 Raising aspirations for further and higher education

> ***"You only get somewhere – e.g. on courses – because people feel sorry for you."*** [8]
> Looked after child

Key information

"The designated teacher should promote a culture in which looked after children believe they can succeed and aspire to further and higher education."

DCSF (2000). Children (Leaving Care) Act: Regulations and Guidance

8 Ofsted (2009). Life in Children's Homes: A Report of Children's Experience by the Children's Rights Director for England

No amount of careful pathway planning can entirely compensate for a lack of motivation on the part of the young person. The pathway plan is there to ensure the care leaver receives support in fulfilling his or her goals, but even formulating these goals is likely to be hampered if the young person has low self-esteem and lacks confidence in his or her ability to achieve good outcomes.[9] This has been identified as particularly damaging in regard to further and higher education, where lack of aspiration may result in the young person either not attempting to apply to university, or lacking the motivation to complete the university course once they have enrolled.

It seems likely that three related causal factors are at work in those children and young people who progress to and stay in university:

- attending a school where other pupils are aiming to go on to university;
- being encouraged by family members or other respected persons; and
- a strong sense of self-motivation.

The challenging task for schools then is to provide individual assistance for looked after children to stimulate and support their individual aspirations for further and higher education, and also to create a culture of high aspirations within the school.

What can individual teachers and members of staff do?

While teachers are right to be realistic about their chances of affecting change in young people's aspirations it should be stressed that the quality of individual teachers' relationships with looked after children or young people is crucial in helping to raise aspirations. Consultation with care leavers has found that the lack of support from teachers is among the key reasons for looked after children and young people losing motivation in their education.[10]

To aid their effectiveness in supporting looked after children in developing aspirations for further and higher education, teachers should:

- take an active interest in the child or young person's educational progress and their plans for the future;
- ensure they understand the opportunities higher education can bring and the various pathways open to young people in continuing education;
- be aware of the relevant member of staff in the school (probably the designated teacher) who can advise them on the looked after child's educational options, and higher education opportunities generally;
- where appropriate involve looked after children and young people in decisions about their educational progress and how it might impact their going on to further and higher education.[11]

What can the school as a whole do?

> ***"It really annoys me that because I'm in care everyone thinks I'm stupid. I try really hard and achieve at school."***[12]
> Looked after child

Schools have to recognise the best way to stimulate aspiration for further and higher education amongst looked after children and young people is to improve their educational attainment, in particular GCSE qualifications. This is likely to be by using the types of targeted support and intervention previously mentioned with a particular emphasis on gaining qualifications that will be useful in further education.

9 Jackson, S., Ajayi S., Quigley, M. (2005). Going to University from Care. London: Institute of Education, p. 17.
10 Allen, M. (2003). Into the Mainstream: Care Leavers Entering Work, Education and Training. York: Joseph Rowntree Foundation, p. 13.
11 On this point see also Munro, E. (2001). Empowering Looked After Children. Child and Family Social Work, vol. 6, no. 2, pp. 129-137.
12 DCSF (2009). Care Matters Ministerial Stocktake Report

In addition there are a number of measures that schools can take to stimulate all children, and particularly looked after children, to progress in education. These include:

- ensure that the senior leadership team and key members of staff such as the designated teacher make progression a whole-school priority;
- consider appointing a separate designated teacher for post-16 students if applicable;
- having good links between key members of staff and class teachers to ensure continuity of approach;
- make sure all teachers are informed about the benefits of higher education and are prepared to be proactive in giving advice and guidance to young people;
- build excellent relationships with parents and carers through involvement in the looked after child's progress and goals; and
- initiate and maintain close relationships with other schools, further and higher education institutions, businesses and third sector organisations, which may be able to offer 'taster' experiences, or provide staff to speak to individuals or groups.[13]

What next?

- Arrange a meeting with the looked after child's class teacher(s) to discuss effective ways to raise aspirations in school.
- Talk to the looked after child about further and higher education, and make sure they have the opportunity to ask questions about what college and university is like. Does he or she have access to the relevant prospectuses? Is he or she aware of any open days they can attend?
- Discuss the possible benefits of the looked after child going on to further and high education with his or her carers, and discuss what can be done at home. If they haven't had personal experience of college or university it may be helpful to send them information, or arrange a meeting to show them round.

8.5 Pathways to further and higher education

The government's Social Exclusion Unit has identified six key challenges to children and young people in care going on to further and higher education:

- lack of qualification and skills;
- insufficient information about the available options;
- poor experiences in school;
- lack of provision of the right kind of courses;
- lack of available transport;
- financial concerns.[14]

There are a number of initiatives currently working to try and reduce the effect of these impediments on looked after children and young people. In particular, those involved with young people in or leaving care should be aware of the different national and local schemes across the public, private and third sectors that offer assistance.

What works well – the Firsbrook Centre, Birmingham

Birmingham has been recognised for its initiatives to build on the education achievements of looked after children, especially those who are hard to reach. For example the Firsbrook Centre has been vital for the looked after children education services. The centre offers shared programmes with mainstream schools to young people who are in part-time education or who are excluded.

Pupils who attend the centre benefit from having the PASS programme (pupil attitude to self and school) which identifies the positive and negative feelings pupils might have, in order to try and reconnect them with learning.

The programme is reviewed every six weeks to follow progress.

Looked after pupils in Birmingham also have the benefit of an 'alternative curriculum coordinator', who

13 Jackson, S., Ajayi S., Quigley, M. (2005). Going to University from Care. London: Institute of Education, p. 17.
14 Social Exclusion Unit (2003). A Better Education for Children in Care. London: Social Exclusion Unit, pp. 29-30.

manages outdoor games and other enjoyable activities such as arts, music, outdoor pursuits, canoeing, climbing, skiing, rollerblading and swimming.

Higher education bursaries

Looked after children and care leavers frequently cite lack of money as an obstacle to their not entering further or higher education.[15] There are various general government schemes designed to help young people cope with the financial burden of further or higher education such as education maintenance Allowance and higher education maintenance grants.

In addition to general provision, the Children and Young Persons Act 2008 specifies that in addition to any other financial assistance local authorities are required to provide all eligible 'former relevant children' (that is, care leavers aged 18-21 who the local authority maintains responsibility for) £2000 towards a higher education course.[16]

For the purposes of the bursary, a 'higher education course' means a course of at least two years duration, conducted at the standard of a first degree (a bachelor of arts, bachelor of science degree, or equivalent). It does not matter for the purposes of the funding whether or not the course is taken full-time or part-time, nor in most cases whether it is a 'distance learning course' (a course completed away from the university campus).

The rate at which the money is paid is largely up to the young person. It may be paid in a lump sum or in instalments throughout the course. If it is paid in instalments, the only caveat is that the last instalment must be paid before the end of the last year of the course, or at the start of the fourth year of the course, whichever comes first. In all matters relating to the higher education bursary, the personal advisor should be able to offer guidance where needed and ensure the money is being received.

The Frank Buttle Trust Quality Mark for Care Leavers in Higher Education

The level of support that higher education institutions provide varies from place to place. A charity called 'The Frank Buttle Trust' has launched a nationwide scheme for parents, carers, professionals and young people to identify those universities that offer superior support for care leavers, of which there are currently 63. Those institutions that meet the criteria set out by the charity will be awarded the Quality Mark.

The Quality Mark indicates the university has made provisions for care leavers and monitors their data regarding former looked after children on an ongoing basis. In particular, the higher education institution must demonstrate their intention to implement these commitments including:

- agreeing a protocol for sharing information including continuing contribution to the pathway plan with the student;
- collecting information about the local authority's financial support for the student with the student's consent;
- if necessary, providing a guarantee for helping the student to confirm accommodation for every day that they are enrolled on their course (including holidays);
- providing personalised and ongoing support including appointing a 'problem solver' for care leavers;
- working with local authorities to raise aspirations for higher education;
- providing the appropriate admissions procedures;
- providing easy access to the relevant financial support;
- ensuring straightforward access to the university's welfare services.[17]

15 Allen, M. (2003). Into the Mainstream: Care Leavers Entering Work, Education and Training. York: Joseph Rowntree Foundation.
16 See the Glossary for the legal definition.
17 The Frank Buttle Trust. 'Higher Education Commitment to Care Leavers'.

A number of universities have now joined the scheme. Even where the care leaver is set to attend a university that has not been awarded the Quality Mark, the above commitments can still be used as a blueprint for good practice.

What works well

Higher education institutions, such as the University of Glamorgan and the University of Southampton, provide additional support for looked after children or care leavers who are still in school but would like a taste of what university is like.

The experiences on offer range from short taster days to week-long summer schools, designed specifically for looked after children to experience student life before becoming a university student. This can be an excellent way to familiarise looked after children with a university setting, and encourage them to meet other looked after children who are prospective university students.

Designated teachers can contact their local university, or the university that the looked after child is thinking of applying to, in order to see what taster experiences they have on offer.

8.6 Pathways to work

Whether through choice or through matters beyond their control, most care leavers in the foreseeable future will not go to university. However, there are a number of initiatives that are available in helping care leavers into employment.

Apprenticeships

Apprenticeships are combined work experience and training placements that offer young people a chance to gain both experience and qualifications in a given job. Apprenticeships run in a number of different industries and should always be paid – currently a minimum of £95 per week, with an average of around £170 every week. They are particularly useful for care leavers as they offer a structured environment in which they can gain knowledge and skills for their future careers whilst enjoying some independence. Generally, apprenticeships run for one to four years.

In 2008, the government made a commitment to offer apprenticeships to all young people leaving care and, from September 2009, there has been a commitment to offer an apprenticeship to every suitably qualified care leaver up to the age of 25. This is set to become a legal entitlement from 2013.[18] Those interested in apprenticeships can contact the National Apprenticeships Service.

From Care2Work

The initiative From Care2Work: Creating Opportunities and Raising Aspirations is a scheme which aims to increase the employability of young people who have left care or are due to leave care soon. It aims to identify good practice and stimulate relationships between corporate parents and employers to increase opportunities for care leavers. The scheme is managed by the National Care Advisory Service (NCAS), a subsidiary of the charity Catch 22, in conjunction with the Department for Education.

The core objectives of the initiative include:

- to work with local authorities to model sustainable employment placements for care leavers;
- to create a quality mark, similar to that of the Frank Buttle Trust to highlight employers that offer support for care leavers;
- to develop work experience programmes to help care leavers to make the transition from care to work.

Since being announced many major employers, including Tesco, O2, Aviva and Marks and Spencer, have signed up to the scheme. This is in addition to over 100 local authorities committing themselves, and a number of government offices and departments giving their support.

18 HM Government (2009). New Opportunities: Fair Chances for the Future. London: The Stationery Office.

Conclusion

The failure to support the development of looked after children has profound impacts on their life chances outside the care system. This chapter has outlined the range of options available post-16 to looked after children, both through the channels open to all young people and through the use of targeted support. Designated teachers may have relatively little contact with looked after children at this stage, depending on the school setting and what choice the child has made. However, knowing the post-16 pathways available to looked after children is important for the designated teacher in laying the foundations for a successful move into adulthood.

What next? Further reading

- Jackson, S. et al. (2005). *Going to University from Care.*
- The government's dedicated website for student funding - www.direct.gov.uk/studentfinance.
- Further information on the Frank Buttle Trust Quality Mark - www.buttletrust.org/quality_mark.
- Care Matters Partnership online resources for designated teachers: www.carematterspartnership.co.uk

Conclusion

This guidebook began by acknowledging that looked after children don't do as well as other children and that this is particularly true in education. The failure to support a looked after child to do well in his or her education will have a profound effect on life chances, in terms on employment, self-esteem and quality of life.

But every looked after child, like every child or young person, is unique and special. The hopes and aspirations of every looked after child will be different and the path to achieving them will be different from one child to another. What makes the difference to each looked after child becoming a success is impossible to say, but it is likely to be a mixture of his or her individual talent and ability, the quality of the care and support provided by the services he or she receives and the inspiration by adults around the child. What is clear, however, is that when done well, the role of the designated teacher can have a powerful influence over all of these aspects of a looked after child's life and can help him or her achieve better results in school.

The information provided here will support any designated teacher - whatever his or her level of experience - to understand the role he or she has in making sure looked after children receive the best education possible. This role must include establishing strong partnerships with other adults in the child's life; ensuring that the educational support needed is being provided to a high standard and that everyone around the child is approaching his or her education with the highest possible expectations and aspirations.

This guidebook has set out:

- the designated teacher's role as set out in legislation and statutory guidance;
- the designated teacher's role in school as part of the network of people and services around the looked after child;
- the role that other services play, and how changes in other areas of the looked after child's life may affect their educational progress and attainment;
- the responsibilities of the local authority broadly and social worker, independent reviewing officer and other specialist services specifically;
- that children come into care for a variety of reasons, and the nature of their care experience will depend upon both their background and the types of care setting into which they are placed;
- the purpose of the child's care plan, including its relationship with the looked after child's health, education, protection and placement;
- how abuse and neglect can affect a looked after child's behavior;
- that relationships with looked after children can take time to establish, but strong engagement on the part of the designated teacher is key to the looked after child's academic, social and emotional development;
- the personal education plan is the key tool for involving all the relevant parties in raising the educational attainment of looked after children;
- the use of extra learning support available to designated teachers to improve the self-confidence of looked after children and bolster educational achievement;
- that looked after children are much more likely than their peers to not be in education, employment or training at the age of 19; and

- the purpose of the pathway plan as the major instrument which is used to ensure the looked after young person's smooth transition out of care.

The knowledge, strategies and skills designated teachers will take from the chapters contained here will hopefully make a big difference, but that alone may not be enough. It will take passion, understanding and dedication to help looked after children fulfil all the potential they have. To be a designated teacher is therefore not something for just any teacher to take on, it needs a special mix of personal skills and attributes.

At times, being a designated teacher will undoubtedly be difficult, but looking at the world from the looked after child's point of view – as this guidebook encourages - will help to put the challenges of the role in some perspective and serve to contextualise its value. Going forward, at times when challenges feel insurmountable, designated teachers and the other professionals working with a looked after child would do well to remind themselves of one simple question; 'what would I do if this were my child?'

Appendix I

Every Child Matters outcomes

Be healthy	• Physically healthy; • mentally and emotionally healthy; • sexually healthy; • healthy lifestyles; • choose not to take illegal drugs.
Stay safe	• *Safe from maltreatment, neglect, violence and sexual exploitation;* • *safe from accidental injury and death;* • *safe from bullying and discrimination;* • *safe from crime and anti-social behaviour in and out of school;* • *have security, stability and are cared for.*
Enjoy and achieve	• *Ready for school;* • *attend and enjoy school;* • *achieve stretching national educational standards at primary school;* • *achieve personal and social development and enjoy recreation;* • *achieve stretching national educational standards at secondary school.*
Make a positive contribution	• *Engage in decision making and support the community and the environment;* • *engage in law-abiding and positive behaviour in and out of school;* • *develop positive relationships and choose not to bully and discriminate;* • *develop self-confidence and successfully deal with significant life changes and challenges;* • *develop enterprising behaviour.*
Achieve economic well-being	• *Engage in further education, employment or training on leaving school;* • *ready for employment;*

Appendix II

National indicators

- NI 50: Emotional health of children
- NI 52: Take up of school lunches
- NI 53: Prevalence of breast-feeding at 6-8 wks from birth
- NI 54: Services for disabled children
- NI 55: Obesity in primary school age children in Reception
- NI 56: Obesity in primary school age children in Year 6
- NI: 57: Children and young people's participation in sporting opportunities
- **NI 62:** The percentage of children looked after at 31 March with three or more placements during the year ending 31 March, by Local Authority
- NI 66: Looked after children cases which were reviewed within required timescales
- NI 68: Percentage of referrals to children's social care going on to initial assessment
- NI 69: Children who have experienced bullying
- NI 71: Children missing from home or care
- NI 72: Achievement of at least 78 points across the Early Years Foundation Stage with at least 6 in each of the scales in Personal Social and Emotional Development and Communication, Language and Literacy.
- NI 73: Achievement at level 4 or above in both English and Maths at Key Stage 2
- NI 75: Achievement of 5 or more A*- C grades at GCSE or equivalent including English and Maths
- NI 76: Reduction in number of schools where fewer than 55% of pupils achieve level 4 or above in both English and Maths at KS2
- NI 78: Reduction in number of schools where fewer than 30% of pupils achieve 5 or more A*- C grades at GCSE and equivalent including GCSEs in English and Maths
- **NI 79**: Achievement of a Level 2 qualification by the age of 19
- NI 80: Achievement of a Level 3 qualification by the age of 19
- NI 81: Inequality gap in the achievement of a Level 3 qualification by the age of 19
- NI 82: Inequality gap in the achievement of a Level 2 qualification by the age of 19
- NI 84: Achievement of 2 or more A*- C grades in Science GCSEs or equivalent
- NI 86: Secondary schools judged as having good or outstanding standards of behaviour
- NI 87: Secondary school persistent absence rate
- NI 88: Percentage of schools providing access to extended services
- NI 89: Reduction of number of schools judged as requiring special measures and improvement in time taken to come out of the category
- NI 90: Take up of 14-19 Learning Diplomas
- NI 91: Participation of 17 year-olds in education or training
- NI 92: Narrowing the gap between the lowest achieving 20% in the Early Years Foundation Stage Profile and the rest.
- NI 93: Progression by 2 levels in English between Key Stage 1 and Key Stage 2
- NI 94: Progression by 2 levels in Maths between Key Stage 1 and Key Stage 2
- NI 102: Achievement gap between pupils eligible for free school meals and their peers achieving the expected level at Key Stages 2 and 4
- NI 103: Special Educational Needs – statements issued within 26 weeks
- NI 104: The Special Educational Needs (SEN)/non-SEN gap – achieving Key Stage 2 English and Maths threshold
- NI 105: The Special Educational Needs (SEN)/non-SEN gap – achieving 5 A*- C GCSE inc. English and Maths.
- NI 107: Key Stage 2 attainment for Black and minority ethnic groups
- NI 108: Key Stage 4 attainment for Black and minority ethnic groups
- NI 109: Delivery of Sure Start Children Centres.
- NI 110: Young people's participation in positive activities
- NI 111: First time entrants to the criminal justice system aged 10-17
- NI 115: Substance misuse by young people
- NI 116: Proportion of children in poverty
- NI 117: 16 to 18 year olds who are not in education, employment or training (NEET)
- NI 199: Children and young people's satisfaction with parks and play areas.

Appendix III

Guide to personal education allowances

What are personal education allowances?
£500 per year for every looked after child that is at risk of not reaching expected levels of educational attainment.

Who qualifies?
Each local authority has responsibility for giving details specific to their locality. The guidance on use of personal education allowances states that pupils are eligible if:

- they are at risk of not reaching the expected national standards (level two in reading, writing and maths at KS1; level four in English and maths at KS2; level five in English and maths at KS3; and five A*-C grades at GCSE, including English and maths, or equivalent;
- they are not expected to make acceptable progress in their education (from the age of seven that means a minimum of two national curriculum levels in English and maths).

Pupils should be eligible whether they are in private, mainstream, residential or kinship care but priority might be given to:

- children in residential care, those placed out of authority;
- recently taken into care (within the last 28 days);
- have experienced multiple school moves;
- have moved school mid-year.

What should the personal education allowance be used for?
Personal education allowances are for supporting looked after children's educational attainment, and they should be put to uses that reflect this. Examples might include:

- personalised educational trips and visits;
- out of school learning and development e.g. music lessons;
- extra tutoring;
- personalised educational trips and visits;
- a PC or laptop with the appropriate software.

Personal education allowance should *not* be used to supplement, pay for or replace activities or items that fall under the remit of existing services or funding streams from local authorities, schools, carers, and other services.

Who decides?
Looked after children should be actively involved in identifying barriers to their learning and in deciding what will help them overcome these challenges and make improved progress with their education. Working out what will help should be part of drawing up the personal education plan, which is done in collaboration with the designated teacher, the social worker, the carers and the young person.
Where the young people have been involved in the decision making process the success of the support is notably higher.

Who decides whether to allocate personal education allowance?_
Each local authority should ideally have a multi-agency panel to decide. In areas where best practice is exemplified around the country this panel has representatives from social work teams, early years, the school, finance departments, corporate parenting panel and of course young people themselves.

What should the personal education allowance be used for?
The government's statutory guidance on personal education allowances sets out the areas of the looked after child's education that the personal education allowance should be spent on, although it leaves considerable flexibility in exactly what services and resources fall into these categories. As the best placed person to assess the learning needs of the looked after child and to consider what extra support they require, the designated teacher plays a central role in personal education allowance decision making.

Glossary

Abuse – a deliberate act of ill-treatment that either causes harm or is liable to cause harm to a child's safety, well-being or development.

Adoption – the process whereby the legal parental rights and responsibilities are transferred to persons other than the child's birth parents.

Attachment – a theory which addresses the nature of the relationship between children and their caregivers; can often be used in relation to looked after children.

Behavioural, emotional and social difficulty (BESD) – can describe pupils who face challenges that present a barrier to their learning, including interaction problems, poor concentration and aggression.

Care leaver – a young person over the age of 16 who has been in the care of the responsible local authority. Those children returning home after being in care are not typically referred to as care leavers. See also 'eligible child', 'relevant child', and 'former relevant child'.

Carer(s) – the person(s) directly responsible for looking after the child. If the child is in residential care this will be carried out by residential care workers; if in foster care, the responsibility will be borne by foster carer(s).

Child and adolescent mental health services (CAMHS) – a team responsible for promoting the mental health and wellbeing of children and young people. Some areas will have specialist CAMHS staff for looked after children.

Child protection register – a list held by each local authority of the children requiring a child protection plan to keep them from harm, co-ordinated by the child's social worker.

Children's home – see 'residential care'.

Children and Young Persons Act 2008 – makes changes to the care planning process and puts extra support for looked after children into law, including the post of designated teacher for looked after children.

Children Act 1989 – makes significant changes to the law regarding all children, including looked after children and children in need. Although amended and supplemented since, it remains the most general legal basis for the care of looked after children.

Children Act 2004 – makes significant changes to the law with the aim of increasing co-operation between different services, including schools and local authorities. Also places a duty on local authorities to promote the educational achievement of looked after children.

Children (Leaving Care) Act 2000 – makes changes to the law regarding the duties that local authorities have to looked after children leaving care, including making it a requirement to provide young people with a personal advisor.

Common Assessment Framework (CAF) – the CAF is a nationally recognised approach for evaluating children's needs, which gives practitioners working with children an effective and consistent means of assessment.

Director of children's services – the senior person in the local authority who is accountable for that authority's services for children, including education, social services for children, and some health functions.

Eligible child – a young person who is 16 or 17 and who has been looked after for at least 13 weeks since the age of 14 and who is still looked after.

Former relevant child – a young person who is aged between 18 and 21 (or is over 21, but still in an agreed programme of education or training) and has been either an eligible child or a relevant child.

Foster care – a care placement for children and young people in a private home.

From Care2Work – a charitable initiative hosted by the National Care Advisory Service aiming to better the outcomes of young people leaving care in terms of education, training and employment.

Independent reviewing officer (IRO) – the person charged with making sure the local authority fulfils their legal duty to each looked after child. Their primary focus lies in quality assuring the care planning process, and making sure the child's views are listened to.

Kinship care – a care placement with a relative or family friend of the child.

Lead member for children's services – a local councillor who has been given responsibility by the Council for children, young people and families.

Looked after child (LAC) – a child or young person who is in the care of their local authority, either because they are subject to a care order, or because they are voluntarily accommodated.

Looked after children education services (LACES) – a team of varying size within the local authority, with responsibility for improving the educational progress and attainment of looked after children within that authority.

Looked after children doctor/nurse – a dedicated staff member within the local authority with responsibility for dealing with the health of looked after children.

Multi-agency working – the act of individuals and groups working together around the looked after child.

National indicators – the set of performance measurements for all local authorities in the country, which allows independent monitoring of their performance.

Neglect – failing to act to secure the basic needs of the child, including his or her physical safety and wellbeing.

Pastoral support plan – a detailed plan concerning the child's behaviour with agreed areas for improvement, aimed at preventing exclusion.

Pathway plan – all looked after children or care leavers over the age of 16 will have a document which sets out how the responsible authority will meet their needs, who will be involved in this process, and when action will be taken.

Personal advisor – the person who co-ordinates the child's pathway plan, and ensures that all the relevant people and services are working to meet its requirements.

Personal education allowance – an annual provision of up to £500 for all looked after children who are at risk of not reaching expected levels of attainment in school.

Personal education plan – the part of the looked after child's care plan regarding his or her learning, which outlines what the child's educational needs are, what is being done to meet these needs, and which people are responsible.

Relevant child – a young person who is 16 or 17 and has been looked after for at least 13 weeks since the age of 14, and has been looked after for some time while they were 16 or 17 and has left care.

Residential care – children's residential care, or children's homes as they are sometimes known, offer a placement for multiple children and provide food, shelter, leisure space and care. They are staffed by residential care workers and support staff.

Responsible local authority – the local authority whose duty it is to care for the looked after child (this is normally, about 70% of the time, the local authority within which the child currently lives).

Safeguarding – the practice of keeping children safe from harm such as illness, abuse or injury including: taking all reasonable measures to ensure risks to children's welfare are minimised and that, where there are concerns, all agencies take appropriate action.

Special educational needs (SEN) – a child is classed as having special educational needs if he or she has a difficulty in learning which means that he or she either: (i) has considerably more difficulty in learning than most of his or her peers of the same age; or (ii) has a disability which partially or wholly restricts use of educational facilities that his or her peers make use of in schools in the local authority area.

Unaccompanied asylum seeking child – a children or young person seeking asylum who does not have a relative or guardian in this country.

Virtual school head (VSH) – a senior person in the local authority who has responsibility for raising the educational attainment and progress of looked after children within schools in that authority.

Whole school approach – a strategy that involves ethos and practice of the wider school community, including teachers, support staff, parents and pupils.

Bibliography

Allen, M. (2003). *Into the Mainstream: Care Leavers Entering Work, Education and Training.* York: Joseph Rowntree Foundation.

Batmanghelidjh C. (2006). *Shattered Lives: Children Who Live with Courage and Dignity.* London: Jessica Kingsley Publishers.

Berridge, D., Henry, L, Jackson, S., and Turney, D (2009). Looked After and Learning: Evaluation of the Virtual School Head Pilot. Nottingham: DCSF Publications.

Bowlby, J (1951). *Child Care and the Growth of Love* Harmondsworth: Penguin.

Brodie, I., Berridge, D., Dobel-Ober, D., and Sinclair, R., (2006). Taking Care of Education. Final Report to the Gatsby Charitable Foundation. London: National Children's Bureau.

Brown, S., and Taylor, K. (2005). Bullying, Education and Labour Market Outcomes: Evidence from the National Child Development Study. Sheffield: Sheffield Economic Research Paper Series.

Brusling C. and Pepin B. (2003) Inclusion in Schools: who is in need of what? *European Educational Research Journal*, vol.2, no. 2.

Caddell, D. (1996). Roles, responsibilities and relationships: Engendering Parental Involvement. Paper presented at the SERA conference Dundee.

Cairns K. (2006). *Attachment, Trauma and Tesilience: Therapeutic Caring for Children.* British Association for Adoption and Fostering.

Care Matters Partnership (2010). *Virtual School Head Journal*, vol.1 Spring 2010.

Corby, B. (2005) *Child Abuse: Towards A Knowledge Base.* Berkshire: Open University Press.

Cummings, C., Dyson, A., Muijs, D., Papps, I., Pearson, D., Raffo, C., Tiplady, L, and Todd, L. (2007). Evaluation of the Full Service Extended Schools Initiative: Final Report. Nottingham: DfES Publications.

CfBT (2006). Information Sharing in Practice: Trainer Notes. CfBT.
Available online at http://www.dcsf.gov.uk/everychildmatters/resources-and-practice/IG00120.

CWDC (2010). Refreshing the Common Core of Skills and Knowledge. Leeds: Children's Workforce Development Council.

CWDC (2010). The Common Core Skills and Knowledge. Leeds: Children's Workforce Development Council.

Davies, L., Williams, C. And Yamashita, H. (2005). Inspiring Schools: Case Studies for Change – Taking up the Challenge of Pupil Participation. Esmée Fairbairn / Carnegie UK Trust.
Available online at:
http://www.esmeefairbairn.org.uk/grants_reports.html#Inspiring_schools.

Dutton, P (2007). Trauma in Children and Young People. Counselling Children and Young People (CCYP).

Every Child a Chance Trust (2006). Every Child a Reader: the First year of the National Roll-out. London: Every Child a Chance Trust.

Fletcher-Campbell, F., Archer, T., and Tomlinson, K. (2004). The Role of the School in Supporting the Education of Children in Public Care. Nottingham: DfES Publications.

Foster, M., (2008). The Role of the Virtual School Head. Sunderland City Council: Item No. 7.
Available online at:
http://www.sunderland.gov.uk/committees/CmisWebPublic/Binary.ashx?Document=8024

Gaskell, C. (2010). If the Social Worker had Called at Least it Would Show they Cared. Young Care Leavers' Perspectives on the Importance of Care. *Children and Society*, vol. 24, no. 2, pp. 136-147.

Geddes H. (2008) Attachment in the Classroom. Kings Lynn: Worth Publishing Ltd.

Geldard, K. (2009). *Practical Interventions for Young People at Risk.* London: Sage Publications.

General Social Care Council (2008). Social Work at its Best: A Statement of Social Work Roles and Tasks for the 21st Century.
Available online at:
http://www.gscc.org.uk/NR/rdonlyres/4EDB6D7E-C18C-4A38-8BEA-D271E9DFFC06/0/RolesandTasksstatementFINAL.pdf

Higgs, J. (2009). *Corporate Parenting: the Contribution of Designated Teachers: Did the Introduction of Designated Teachers for Looked After Children Improve their Educational Achievements and Outcomes? Berlin:* VDM Verlag Dr. Muller Aktiengesellschaft & Co. KG.

Home Office: Immigration and Nationality Directorate (2007). Planning Better Outcomes and Support for Unaccompanied Asylum Seeking Children: Consultation Paper. The Home Office.

House of Commons, Children, Schools and Families Committee (2009). Looked-after Children: Third Report of Session 2008-9, Volume 1. London: The Stationery Office.

HM Government (2006). Working Together to Safeguard Children: A guide to Inter-agency Working to Safeguard and Promote the Welfare of Children. London: The Stationery Office.

HM Government (2009). New Opportunities: Fair Chances for the Future. London: The Stationery Office.

Jackson, S. (1994). Educating Children in Residential and Foster Care. *Oxford Review of Education*, vol. 20, no. 3, pp. 267-79.

Jackson, S. (2006). Looking after children away from home, past and present in Chase, Simon and Jackson (eds.) *In Care and After: a Positive Perspective.* Abingdon: Routledge.

Jackson, S., Ajayi S., Quigley, M. (2005). *Going to University from Care.* London: Institute of Education.

Joughin, C (2006). Evidence Nugget: Cognitive behaviour therapy can be effective in managing behavioural problems and conduct disorder in pre-adolescence. What Works for Children group: Evidence Nugget.

Kirby, P., Lanyon, C., Cronin, K. and Sinclair, R. (2003). Building a Culture of Participation: Involving children and Young People in Policy: Service Planning, Delivery and Evaluation. Nottingham: DfES Publications.

Knowles, G. (2009). *Ensuring Every Child Matters: A Critical Approach.* London: Sage Publications.

Leicester County Council. Foster Carers' Responsibilities.
Available online at: http://www.leics.gov.uk/2.1_foster_carers_responsibilities.pdf

Meltzer, H., Gatward, R., Corbin, T., Goodman, R. and Ford, T. (2003). The Mental Health of Young People Looked After by Local Authorities in England. Norwich: HMSO.

Munro, E. (2001). Empowering Looked After Children. Child and Family Social Work, vol. 6, no. 2, pp. 129-137.

NCB (2006). Understanding Why: Understanding Attachment and How this Can Affect Education with Special Reference to Adopted Children and Young People and Those Looked After by Local Authorities. London: National Children's Bureau.

NASUWT and DfES (2006). School Discipline: Your Rights and Powers as a Teacher', Nottingham: DfES Publications.

NCAS (2009). Journeys to Home: Care leavers' successful transition to independent accommodation. London: National Care Advisory Service.

Office for Disability Issues (2010). Models of Disability.
Available online at:
http://www.officefordisability.gov.uk/resources/models-of-disability.php

Ofsted (2007). Children's Messages on Care: A Report by the Children's Rights Director for England. London: Ofsted.

Ofsted (2008) Looked After Children – Good Practice in Schools. London: Ofsted.

Ofsted (2009). Quality and Standards in Care, Early Education, Schools, Colleges, Adult Learning and Skills, and Children's Services: The Annual Report of Her Majesty's Chief Inspector 2008/09. London: Ofsted.

Ofsted (2009). Life in Children's Homes: A Report of Children's Experience by the Children's Rights Director for England. London: Ofsted.

Royal College of Psychiatrists (2004). Child Abuse and Neglect: the Emotional Effects. Factsheet for Parents and Teachers. Mental Health and Growing Up, Factsheet 19. London: Royal College of Psychiatrists.

Sandringham Primary School (2010). Looked After Children Policy 2010. Available online at: http://webfronter.com/newham/Sandringham_Primary_School/menu5/Safeguarding_Your_Child/images/Looked_After_Children_policy_2010.pdf

Sinclair, I., Baker, C., Lee, J. and Gibbs, I. (2007). *The Pursuit of Permanence: A Study of the English Child Care System'* London: Jessica Kingsley Publishers.

Social Exclusion Task Force (2009). Realising Young Potential: Supporting Care Leavers Into Education, Employment and Training. London: Cabinet Office.

Social Exclusion Unit (2003). A Better Education for Children in Care. London: Social Exclusion Unit.

Social Services Committee, Second Report of Session 1983–84. Children in care: HC 360.

Steer, A. (2009). Learning Behaviour: Lessons Learned. A Review of Behaviour Standards and Practices in our Schools. London: DCSF Publications.

The Frank Buttle Trust. 'Higher Education Commitment to Care Leavers'.
Available online at:
http://www.buttletrust.org/fncms_orphan/click_here_to_find_out_more_about_the_quality_mark/?orphan_parent_id=87.

Whitney, B. (1993). The Children Act and Schools. London: Kogan Page.
Who Cares? Trust (2010). Charlotte's Story. Available online at: http://www.thewhocarestrust.org.uk/pages/charlottes-story.html.

Government Legislation, Regulations and Guidance

Adoption and Children Act 2002, (c. 38). London: HMSO.

Care Standards Act 2000, (c. 14). London: HMSO.

Children Act 1989, (c. 41). London: HMSO.

Children Act 2004, (c.31). London: HMSO.

Children and Young Persons Act 2008, (c. 20). London: HMSO.

Children Leaving Care Act 2000, (c. 35). London: HMSO.

DCSF (2007). Children's Plan: Building Brighter Futures. London: The Stationery Office.

DCSF (2008). Every Child Matters Outcomes Framework. Nottingham: DCSF Publications.

DCSF (2008). Improving Behaviour and Attendance: Guidance on Exclusion from Schools and Pupil Referral Units. Nottingham: DCSF Publications.

DCSF (2008). Information Sharing Pocket Guide. Nottingham: DCSF Publications.

DCSF (2008). Personal Education Allowances for Looked After Children: Statutory Guidance for Local Authorities. Nottingham: DCSF Publications.

DCSF (2008). Targeted Mental Health in Schools Project, Using the Evidence to Inform Your Approach: A Practical Guide for Headteachers and Commissioners. Nottingham: DCSF Publications.

DCSF (2008). Working Together: Listening to the Voices of Children and Young People. Nottingham: DCSF Publications.

DCSF (2009). Care Matters: Ministerial Stocktake Report 2009. Nottingham: DCSF Publications.

DCSF (2009). Children Looked After in England (Including Adoption and Care Leavers) Year Ending 31 March 2009: Statistical First Release. Nottingham: DCSF Publications.

DCSF (2009). Improving the Educational Attainment of Children In Care (Looked After Children). Nottingham: DCSF Publications.

DCSF (2009). Improving the Attainment of Looked After Children in Primary Schools: Guidance for Schools. Nottingham: DCSF Publications.

DCSF (2009). Improving the Attainment of Looked After Children in Secondary Schools: Guidance for Schools. Nottingham: DCSF Publications.

DCSF (2009). The Role and Responsibilities of the Designated Teacher for Looked After Children: Statutory Guidance for School Governing Bodies. Nottingham: DCSF Publications.

DCSF (2010). Breaking the Link Between Special Educational Needs and Low Attainment: Everyone's Business. Nottingham: DCSF Publications.

DCSF (2010). Guidance on Commissioning Targeted Mental Health and Emotional Wellbeing Services in Schools. Nottingham: DCSF Publications.

DCSF (2010). The Children Act 1989 Guidance and Regulations Volume 2: Care Planning, Placement and Case Review. Nottingham: DCSF Publications.

DCSF (2010). The Pupil and Parent Guarantees. Nottingham: DCSF Publications.

DCSF and DoH (2009). Improving the psychological wellbeing and mental health of children and young people. Nottingham: DCSF Publications.

DfES (2001). Special Educational Needs: Code of Practice. Nottingham: DfES Publications.

DfES (2004). Pedagogy and Practice: Teaching and Learning in Secondary Schools. Nottingham: DfES Publications.

DfES (2005) Children in Need in England: Results of a Survey of Activity and Expenditure as Reported by Local Authority Social Services' Children and Families Teams for a Survey Week in February 2005: Local Authority Tables and Further National Analysis (Internet only).
Available online at:
http://www.dcsf.gov.uk/rsgateway/DB/VOL/v000647/index.shtml

DfES (2005). Common Core of Skills and Knowledge for the Children's Workforce. Nottingham: DfES Publications.

DfES (2005). Statutory Guidance on the Duty on Local Authorities to Promote the Educational Achievement of Looked After Children under Section 52 of the Children Act 2004. Nottingham: DfES Publications.

DfES (2006). Care Matters: Transforming the Lives of Children and Young People. London: The Stationary Office.

DfES (2006). Future Positive: A Resource Guide for People Working With Disabled Care Leavers. London: The Stationery Office.
DfES (2006). Implementing the Disability Discrimination Act in School and Early Years Settings. Nottingham: DfES Publications.

DfES (2006). Who Does What: How Social Workers and Carers Can Support the Education of Children in Care. Nottingham: DfES Publications.

DfES (2007). Care Matters: Time for Change. London: The Stationery Office.

DfES (2007). Pedagogy and Personalisation: Primary and Secondary National Strategies. Nottingham: DfES Publications.

DfES (2004). Aiming High: Guidance on Supporting the Education of Unaccompanied Asylum Seeking Children, A Guide To Good Practice. Nottingham: DfES Publications.

DoH (1991). An Adviser's Guide to the Children Act. London: Department of Health.

DoH (1991). Working Together Under the Children Act. London: Department of Health.

DoH (2001). Children (Leaving Care) Act 2000: Regulations and Guidance. London: Department of Health.

DoH (2002). Fostering Services: National Minimum Standards, Fostering Services Regulations. London: The Stationery Office.

DoH and DfEE (2000). Guidance on the Education of Children in Public Care. London: DfEE.

Special Educational Needs and Disability Act (SENDA) 2001, (c. 10). London: HMSO.

The Designated Teacher (Looked After Pupils etc)(England) Regulations 2009. London: HMSO.

The Disability Discrimination Act 1995, (c. 50). London: HMSO.

The School Admissions (Adjudicator Determinations Relating to Looked After and Certain Other Children) (England) Regulations 2007, (Statutory Instrument, no. 105). London: HMSO.